George Mostardini

LIFE IS A FIGHT

Memoirs of a Boxer

Chicago, 2017

To LINDA

To my beautiful wife Ellen, for all your help with this project
and every other project in my life.

To my children Gina, Lisa and George for all your understanding
and to my grandchildren Christina, Abby, Anthony and Vivian.

To my parents George and Ann, to my trainer and friend DeeDee
Armour, to Ernie Terrell for all your support, to my best friend
Kip, I will always miss you. Unfortunately they are no longer
with us but will forever remain in my heart. May you all
rest in peace.

To Dr. Alexander Golbin, for encouraging me to stay calm, cool
and keep writing.

To all – may any demons you have go far away.

Contents

Images

Chapter One

When I was eighteen, I was drafted into the Army, where despite the whole buddy system they preached, it was basically every man for himself. I did everything I could to avoid real work. At one point, we had to take apart our rifles and clean every inch of them. Come inspection time, my bunkmate's rifle parts were spotless, so I switched his for mine. After inspection, Top Bunk figured it out who screwed him over, and he was *pissed* and came after me looking for a fight. He was maybe twenty-three years old and a big guy, about 6'4" and 240 lbs., while I was about 6' and 165 lbs. This is where my boxing training came in—discipline, stamina, looking for weak spots and openings. I couldn't believe how young men could be so out of shape, how naïve, with little to no street smarts to comical proportions at times. Top Bunk came after me, but I beat him so bad, he had to go to the infirmary. I will say this: to his credit, Top Bunk was no snitch. Everyone in the barracks was impressed, so now I could use the same bullying tactics on just about everyone else, which I took advantage of to get through and complete basic training. After I got home, I got a job working for the gas company, but I had to go to training camp for two weeks every summer for six years.

I was almost out three years when my girlfriend, Ellen, became pregnant. It wasn't too big a deal since we had already been together six years and were planning on getting married anyway, but it was hard on both of us when we first got married because we were broke. Even though I worked two jobs and Ellen had a part-time job, things were tight. One of my get-rich-quick schemes was to become a professional boxer. I was always getting into fights, so a friend suggested I try boxing, probably make a lot of cash. Well, I went for it. I always dreamed of fighting in the ring, always. It was deep in my head that I could become a great fighter, so I went for it.

I was a pretty good athlete in grammar school and high school, and boxing always intrigued me—I just never knew how to get involved in the sport. A friend of mine felt the same, so one day we decided to go down to the Catholic Youth Organization gym on Jackson Street near downtown Chicago. C.Y.O. had two general trainers for everyone, Leo Ranere and Frank Shields, just two guys volunteering their time to keep kids off the street.

They taught me all the fundamentals of boxing: how to train, jump rope, punch right—everything to get ready for a fight. What I remember most is that controlling teenagers from going all out was impossible, so we sparred like it was a real fight. In a couple of months, we were prepared for our first amateur fights. About thirty or thirty-five amateur fights later, I won the park district novice championship at light heavyweight, a proud moment in my amateur career.

Once I decided to give pro boxing a try, I started training at the fireman's gym at Navy Pier, which was mostly for basketball players but had all the essentials for boxing: heavy bags, speedbags, and a ring. That's all a boxer needs to start with, but the first step for a fighter is to get in good shape, and running was the perfect start. The first day I started to train, I got up at five that morning and went out jogging, slowly around the baseball field where I used to play little league baseball for North Elm Youth Baseball. For one week, I slowly jogged around the park, throwing in a few sprints now and then, and followed with sit-ups, push-ups, leg raises until I was sore. Many times I thought to myself, *Why in the hell are you doing this?* I thought of all the times I'd fucked up in my life, that maybe, just maybe, I could redeem myself. But I knew in my heart it wouldn't make any difference to all the people I hurt or let down. So every morning I kept at it. After work I would pick up my trainer, Carlo Sarlo, to go to the gym and work, work, work. I was tired and exhausted from working all day, but I continued to think I could redeem myself as a boxer, so I kept going, every day, over and over. It took a good six weeks to get back into shape just to get into the ring.

I remember my first sparring session was about three rounds with a guy named Tony who'd had three pro fights with a record of 1-1-1. This was my first time back in the ring since my amateur days. Tony thought it was just a sparring match, but to me it was a real fight. Anytime I put the gloves on and someone was in front of me, it was him or me—just how I was taught at the C.Y.O. The round started and I caught him by surprise with my aggressiveness, winging punches from all angles as hard as I could. Tony was mostly on the defense for two rounds, but by the third round I was exhausted and could hardly finish. When we were done, Tony had a bloody nose, and I didn't learn anything I didn't already know before: fight for your life.

This went on for about a month until Ernie Terrell came to the gym one day to spar with me. Ernie was a former heavyweight champ and was now promoting fights in Chicago. He wanted to put me on one of his fight cards, so he wanted to see what I had. I was honored, of course, and learned more in those three rounds sparring with him than I had ever learned before. I actually had three fights before in Oklahoma City, winning two by KO and the third was a four-round decision, and a fight scheduled in Orlando, Florida, the next week, but I really had no idea what I was doing, just throwing bombs and hoping for the best.

After the fight in Orlando, which I won by KO, Ernie came back to Navy Pier and told me I should come down and train at his gym, Woodlawn Boys Club, because there were more boxers and better boxers to spar with. I took his advice and went down there on a random day, but when I showed up, I saw it was basically empty. Ernie came out and said, "Are you crazy? It's Martin Luther King Day, and this isn't exactly the right place for a white guy to be today!" It never even crossed my mind, but Ernie still put on his gear and sparred four rounds with me. He then introduced me to an old black guy, DeeDee Armour, a trainer and explained that DeeDee could show me more in a week than I had learned in the last six months. Ernie was right. DeeDee taught me to throw a punch in the right way, not just wing it. He taught me footwork, defense, and a whole lot of tricks for my arsenal. Most importantly, he taught me to relax,

9

not be so tense all the time: "When you're tense, you get tired quickly and your punches don't flow as easily. Your body needs to relax so your reflexes move quicker and smoothly." So began a long friendship with my new trainer.

DeeDee was once an amateur and pro fighter but without much success. Still, he wanted to stay in the fight game, so he studied it and became a successful trainer. The first thing he said to me was, "I know one thing is for sure, I know you have balls because there hasn't been a white guy in this gym for a long, long time."

Once DeeDee and I stated training together, he changed my entire style of boxing. He taught me how to throw straight, hard punches, defense, footwork, how to get out of trouble in the ring, even tricks of the trade. When I started fighting, he was the one constant in my corner and knew every little thing for the advantage. We used eight-oz. gloves with horse hair for padding, and DeeDee told me to keep hitting the wall to move the padding down to my fingers so my knuckles would be closer to the leather. It always seemed like DeeDee knew what my opponent was thinking, and when I would go back to my corner between rounds, he always gave me the right directions and corrections.

More than a trainer, DeeDee was like a father to me and watched out for me. If I couldn't make it to the gym for some reason, I felt like a kid trying to explain it to him. He made me weigh in almost every day to make sure I was keeping in shape, and he always felt the pain I felt when it came to losses, bad decisions, cuts and bruises. In between rounds, before I walked back to the center of the ring, we would always bump fists— DeeDee's way of showing me he was always with me.

I miss his friendship most of all. He was a great trusted friend, and we spent many hours talking about life itself, not just boxing. My best times with DeeDee were mostly after a fight, when I would drive him home. He lived above a tavern on the South Side of Chicago, and the drive gave us time to talk. He was always positive whether I won or lost and would always give me encouragement, reaffirming certain things that I could learn from every fight. Once we arrived at his apartment we would go to the tavern for a drink, and he would always have a couple shots of Crown Royal bourbon. Even though I was the only white guy in the place, everyone knew DeeDee trained me, and they would all stand up and cheer, especially after a good win.

The next day I went down to Ernie's gym and sparred with a fighter named Walter Moore. Walter was already a ten-round pro fighter and usually fought the main event on Ernie's fight card. Well, the fact that I was a white guy in a black man's gym didn't go over so well with some of the guys working out there. Walter was one of them, and he let me know it—he gave me an old-fashioned beating for four rounds. He and the others were all a little surprised when I showed up again the next day, and he continued to beat the shit out of me every time we sparred. I took my beatings like a man without complaints, but I learned something from every session. It took some time but after a while I earned a small measure of respect. As time went on and I improved, I became the better fighter. Sparring one day with Moore, I caught him on the chin with a left hook; he had head gear on and it still knocked him out. It ended his career, and he never came back to the gym.

I had a goal and a dream, and I was not going to be stopped.

Chapter Two

In October 1977, I had my first fight in Chicago at the Aragon Ballroom. I remember seeing my name on the marquee as I walked down Lawrence Ave, and I thought to myself, *Yeah, that's me, and everyone else is going to see it, too.* I even circled the building to see all three sides of the marquee with my name, all lit up. I had driven past this place many times before, seeing concerts advertised there, and there it was now, my name. "GEORGE MOSTARDINI VS. TROY BOLDEN." But along with my name in lights came the pressure to win. *If I lose, I'm gonna look like an idiot.* I'd had two fights in Orlando and three in Oklahoma City, but this would be my first at home. I was scheduled to fight a four-round bout against Troy Bolden, a former Golden Glove heavyweight champion. I had seen him train at the Woodlawn Boys Club, but he came in at different hours. As the only white guy at an otherwise black training club, I was an outsider, so Bolden and a handful of other guys took it out on me whenever we sparred.

All my friends, all my family, and anyone who knew me at the time took buses from bars all over the city to the Aragon that night. Ernie was promoting the fight, and he was extremely excited because the fight was sold out. His previous promotions got maybe twelve to fifteen hundred people, but this fight sold out a full house, with anywhere from forty-five hundred to five thousand people, as many as the Aragon could hold. In the front row, with his beautiful wife and holding his baby daughter Hana, was Muhammad Ali.

Ernie and Ali hated each other at one time. Ali lost his title as the only U.S. heavyweight champion and his license to fight in the States because he dodged the draft, but he could still fight in Europe and Canada. The European and Canadian boxing commissions granted special permission for a WBA Heavyweight tournament in 1965, knowing it would bring in big money, and eight fighters competed for the title. Ernie Terrell beat Eddie Machen in Chicago for the title and defended his title two more times after that, once against George Chuvalo in Toronto and then Doug Jones in Houston, all by fifteen-round decisions. Then on February 6, 1967, Muhammed received his license back and Ernie and Muhammad were scheduled to fight in the Astrodome to unify the titles.

Ernie insisted on calling Ali "Cassius Clay" during all the press conferences, which Ali took great offense to since he considered "Clay" to be his slave name. But Ernie kept it up, and Ali said he would "give him a whuppin' come fight time. During the fight, Ernie continued to call him "Cassius," and Ali kept jamming his thumb in Ernie's left eye while taunting him, yelling, "What's my name now, nigger, what's my name now?" Ali won the fight by a fifteen-round decision, but Ernie claimed he fought dirty by trying to blind him. Even though they both lived in Chicago, they didn't speak to each other for years after the fight, but when Ernie started promoting fights in the city, he and Ali buried the hatchet.

Ernie wasn't making much money on the previous fights, but when he booked me in October, he couldn't print tickets fast enough. I had a huge group of followers who were just waiting for me to fight at home. Ticket sales were going great, better than Ernie had ever expected, and the Aragon would be filled to the brim. That's when Ernie asked Ali to make a special surprise appearance at the fight. Ali, always the showman, got a kick out of it—he could always draw attention and knew how to put on a show, and I think he felt a little guilty for what he did to Ernie years earlier in that fight. Ali came to the Aragon that night with his wife and daughter Hana, and Ernie was thrilled.

That night, before the fight, Muhammad came to talk to me in my dressing room., Ali asked me what made me start fighting, how much I weighed, how tall I was, telling me I was in great shape. I think he was

13

curious about the guy whose name was all over the marquee. Ali joked around a lot, mugging his face like he would do. As he left, he wished me good luck and commented about my great following of fans, joking that they must be mob guys with machine guns.

Since most people got to the fight by organizing bus trips from bars, by the time it started they were three sheets to the wind. I was nervous because it was not only my first fight in Chicago but also my first time with DeeDee as the main trainer in my corner. I remember going to the ring with deafening cheers headed my way. I saw my father, who was always more nervous than me before fights, in the second row and gave him a wink. With all my friends and family coming, there was so much hype about the fight. But once I got into the ring, my head cleared and I forgot all about the crowd.

Across the ring was Troy Bolden, the guy that didn't think I deserved to train in the same gym as him. He didn't like me, which was fine with me because I couldn't stand the jerkoff either. All I wanted was to knock his ass out and show him what I'd learned since coming to "his" gym. I took a look at him in his corner. He was about 5'10", 220 lbs., with a belly on him and a scowl on his face that I guess was supposed to scare the shit out of me.

The bell rings, and it's on.

He comes out with both hands at his waist, trying to shuffle around like Ali. He thinks he's cool and trying to show he's not afraid. I stand up straight and look about six inches taller than him. I throw two jabs that knock him back on his heels, and his hands come up right away. He clinches, but I easily shake him off. I throw a right, left, right, left to his body—every punch lands solid. After two minutes of this we get into a slugging match. We both land a half dozen punches, but my last two punches, a looping right and a left hook, land solidly against his head, and down he goes. As he falls, his head bounces off the bottom rope, and he's out cold. The referee counts to ten—2:38 into the first round, I get a clean KO.

The crowd erupts, standing, screaming, like nothing I had ever seen. I had a shit-eating grin as Bolden's corner men help him into his corner. As I walked around the ring with my arms raised, I caught a glimpse of Ali. He was shouting, throwing air punches at me with that frown on his face, the way he liked to fool around. So I played around with him, throwing my arms up at him to come in the ring, and he had his body guards pretend to hold him back. The fans loved it. Everyone thought it was all a prepared act, but it was just classic Ali, who always liked to be the center of attention—and it worked. It was great publicity for me because it was in all the papers the next day, and Ernie was beaming. That night, Ernie had already scheduled another fight for me in four weeks.

DeeDee told me, "Take the weekend off, and I'll see you on Monday. Don't let your head get too big over this one bout. The fights are going to get harder and the fighters tougher. Come in on Monday prepared to work." He added, "I'm proud of you for tonight's fight. Make me proud of you again in four weeks." DeeDee was right. I couldn't let this get to me. After the fight, Ali came to my dressing room again to congratulate me and told me he would be following me in the future. After the fight I went to Hoagies Pub on North Ave. for a great steak and a few beers with all my friends and family.

Ali and I spoke again two months later, when I fought an eight-round bout while Ali fought Scott Ledoux in a five-round. He asked me how things were going and told me to keep up the good work, joking, "Maybe if I stick around long enough, we'll meet in the ring."

Chapter Three

The year 1978 was a memorable one for me. I was working my way up the chain after winning two second-round KOs, and it was time to move to eight-round bouts, which meant much better and tougher competition. At the time, everyone wanted to see me fight two other popular fighters in Chicago: Baker Tinsley from Louisville, Kentucky, and Tom "Ruffhouse" Fischer from Dayton, Ohio. Fischer had won an eight-round decision over Tinsley, and my next fight was to be an eight-rounder against Tinsley at the Aragon. If I won, my next fight would be against Ruffhouse. This was really the fight everyone wanted to see because Ruffhouse and I were both crowd favorites, but I had to get past Tinsley first, who wasn't a bad fighter himself. The fight with Tinsley was one of the most savage fights I ever had.

The bell rings for Round One, and he comes at me with a roundhouse right hand. I roll my left shoulder in, just like DeeDee trained me, and the punch lands on my bicep, exactly how DeeDee and I had practiced. The next move is to fire a straight right hand, so I catch him straight on the chin and down he goes, like perfection. Tinsley is back on his feet at the count of five, but he takes the entire eight count to get ready, and war is on. He's hurt and desperate, so I have to be careful. In moments like these, getting aggressive is like cornering a wild animal that will do anything to survive. I catch him with a left hook and another right hand, and then I catch him with the widow maker, a left hook to the liver followed by at least eight unanswered punches, and down he goes again. This time it's over—he's out for five minutes.

Fight fans are nothing more than fucking animals. They go berserk as Tinsley crumples to a heap and grow even louder when they see he isn't moving. This is what they paid money for: they want blood, they want vicious KOs. They love it when the doctors take a fighter out on a stretcher. The more they think someone is seriously hurt, the more they cheer. Who cares about Baker Tinsley?

This is a big win for me, a great night, but now I have to fight Tom Fischer.

The fight was set for the end of May. Ernie knew this fight would draw too many people for the Aragon, so he booked the fight at the International Amphitheatre for the first time. In its heyday, the International Amphitheatre held conventions, concerts, monster car shows, roller derby along with wrestling and boxing matches. Holding a fight here was a big deal and meant it would draw a larger crowd which meant more money and more publicity.

In the months leading up to it, my local celebrity status grew gradually. Car dealer Joe Perillo owned a Pontiac dealership at the time, and he asked me if I was interested in starring in a TV commercial for $1,000 and a brand new Pontiac Bonneville I could drive for one year. I would have been crazy not to do it, so, of course, I agreed. Perillo wanted to shoot the commercial at the Woodlawn Boys Club, which I wasn't too happy about because I didn't want the other fighters to think I was some kind of Prima Donna, but the shoot actually went very well, and the director let the other fighters and some neighborhood kids be in the background of the commercial. Perillo gave out T-shirts and $20 to everyone who participated, so they were all happy as could be. The commercial aired on Channel 26, which needed rabbit ears, which was an antenna to watch television in the days before cable or satellite dish. There were really only four prime time channels at the time, plus Channels 11, 26, and 32. We filmed three different commercials, all of which would not be on the prime channels, but channel 26 still had a pretty fair amount of programming, so seeing myself on the air was really something. Next was a live Sunday morning talk show with 36th Ward Alderman Lou Farini, who interviewed people from the neighborhood every Sunday morning on Channel 26. I was very nervous while doing the show, but Farini guided me through every step of the way. We talked about my boxing career, where it was headed, boxing, as a sport and my family. Not only did I have a thousand bucks in my pocket and was driving a brand new Pontiac Bonneville, but I was seen by everyone in Chicago. Even after all this I still wasn't through being a celebrity.

I knew all the publicity was necessary, but I never like being in that kind of lime light. I just wanted to fight and leave all the publicity to my manager. One of my biggest fans at the time was Channel 7 sports anchor Tim Weigel. He'd been at every one of my Chicago fights and always had great things to say about me on the news. A few days before the fight, he interviewed Fischer and me live at the Navy Pier firemen's gym for the ten o'clock news. Fischer and I gave our predictions on how the fight would come out (naturally, we both predicted that we would win). After the interview, Tim asked me if I would punch him in the stomach. I wasn't sure if he was fooling around and told him I could hurt him, but Tim reassured me, "I brought this big encyclopedia book with me and I'll put it under my shirt." I agreed, but I didn't want to take the chance I would hurt him and hit him at half strength. Still, Tim played it up and pretended to fly up against the ring post. All this press was great but it put a tremendous amount of pressure on me to win this fight. After all this exposure, how would it look if I lost? I would be humiliated. I was tense for this fight like never before.

That night, we were the main event and scheduled for eight rounds. I'd never been past four rounds, and Fischer was no slouch—his record at the time was 19:2 against good fighters, and he'd never been KO'd—so the odds were I was going all eight rounds.

The Amphitheatre was jam packed that night, with standing room only. I was nervous as a cat during all the preliminary bouts. My friends, family, even classmates all the way back to grammar school showed up for the fight, so the pressure was on. When the prelims were over, my team and I headed down to the ring. Still I couldn't shake off the nervousness. I could see how crowded it was, and the crowd's growing noise meant they were drinking. I looked around and spotted my father right off the row of seats by my corner. I gave him a wink to let him know that everything was going to be alright.

Just before the fight, the National Anthem starts playing. This was always puzzling to me, why they wait until the main event to sing the National Anthem when all other sports sing it before the start of the event. It's funny what goes through your head right before you go to war with someone you really have nothing against.

The bell rings for Round One, and Ruffhouse comes out at me with a right hand. I freeze up, forget to roll my left shoulder, and get hit in the face. Pressure can make you forget the things that should have come naturally from all my training. But he uses his Sunday punch, which doesn't hurt me; instead, it wakes me up and makes me feel like he can't hurt me too bad. All the pressure falls away and I go to work. I'm taller than Tom and have a longer reach, so I jab left, right , left. I keep him back so he can't get another hard punch like the first one. He goes for my body, but I easily shove him back and see I'm stronger than him, too. His strategy is to crowd me to make up for his shorter reach. Although the round ends pretty even, I feel good and confident. *I'm in good shape, I've trained hard.* I get back to my corner, and DeeDee says, "Roll with the right, and when he tries to crowd you, use the upper cut."

Round Two starts, and again he comes in. This time, instead of pushing him off, I fire a right uppercut and a left hook—perfect strategy, and I catch him clean with both shots. He comes back at me and I use my jab and ram right and left uppercuts on him. I can see he's confused, his head is down and he doesn't change his fight style, so I keep it up. The second round is easily mine, and DeeDee tells me to pressure him, that I am hurting him. So I keep it up in the third round, and I feel good but I'm bothered by one thing. *Why he doesn't change his strategy? Does he have a trick up his sleeve? What surprise does he have in store?* The third round is mine again, and I figure the score is 2:1 in my favor. DeeDee tells me to step it up again.

Round Four starts and I go after him. After I land a solid right uppercut and a left hook, I fire a hard left hook to the body, and he stumbles against the ropes, which the referee rules a knockdown. Fischer has eight seconds to get back up, and as I wait in a neutral corner, my corner team screams at me to go right after him again. I listen and hit the top of his head with my right hand—pain shoots right up to my shoulder. I immediately think that I broke my hand (forty years later, the middle knuckle on my right hand is still three times the size of my left). Fischer clinches and I lose my chance at a knockout, but he's still hurt. Injured fighters often improvise until some of the pain subsides, so I use my left hand to easily win the round. I return to my corner and my team yells, "Why did you let up?!" I tell them I think I busted my hand, so DeeDee says to keep using the left and use the right as a decoy, not to throw it full power.

The fifth round starts, no man's land for me, and I work the jab. When Fischer comes in close, I use my strength to push him off and work the body, just like during the first round. My right hand is starting to feel better towards the end of the round, but the bout is still close and can go either way. I figure the absolute worst case is that I was scoring 3:2. I get to my corner and tell DeeDee my right hand feels pretty good, so he tells me go back and pour it on. In the sixth round, I go back to the upper cuts and take control again. I'm still wondering why Fischer doesn't change his strategy. *Maybe he can't?* I win the round easily and the score 4:2 for me, plus I've got an extra point for the knockdown.

The seventh starts and I take control for the first two and a half minutes. I've thrown a ton of punches at this guy, but suddenly I hit a wall: I'm getting tired. Exhausted really. The worst situation is being tired when your opponent isn't. There isn't anyone else to take your place. There is no team, no time out, and it's harder and harder to keep going. I manage to win this round, but I still have the last round to worry about, and I'm getting gassed. DeeDee gives me four or five squirts of his "special "water and in just a few seconds I can feel my lungs open up. I can breathe again. I look at Fischer's corner, and he looks pretty fresh to me. I think, maybe that's his plan, to wait for me to burn out. DeeDee tells me to keep using my jab and when Fischer comes in, clinch. This gives me a little time to rest. I have great faith in DeeDee and follow his orders to a tee, but Fischer pounds me around in the last round, and I know I've lost this round. At this point I'm sucking wind, so I'm grateful to hear the bell.

Now we wait for the decision. The pressure to win from all the media had my stomach in knots for the last ten days. Now it's over and I feel that I have won. They announce the scores and I win a unanimous decision: two judges by three points, one judge by four points. So those two close rounds mostly went to Fischer, just goes to show that judges sometimes see the fight a different way. Still, I heave a great sigh of relief and look forward to relaxing with my family for a few days before going back to the gym.

After the fight I talked with Fischer for ten minutes or so. The man took a great punch and had incredible stamina to keep on coming. He was a huge crowd favorite in Chicago and definitely the hardest fight I had so far. I found out we had a bit in common. We both made a living in manual labor full-time, I as a construction worker and he as a carpet layer, but we worked just as hard, if not harder, to be professional boxers. Later in my career, I fought in Kentucky five times, and Fischer was on the same fight card every time: once in Louisville, where Michael Spinks fought the main event, and four times in Covington, where Fischer was the main event. Tom and I ended up being good friends. Funny how boxing works.

One day, you're trying to kill a perfectly decent guy, and the next day you're having a drink with him after fighting each other's opponents.

Most people don't realize the sacrifices a fighter makes to follow their dream. Fighters give everything they have in their heart and soul to win the heavyweight championships; 99.5% fail to achieve this goal—it's that half percent that keeps giving their all.

Chapter Four

In 1978, Ernie asked me, "How would you like to be the one to fight in an exhibition with Leon Spinks, Heavyweight Champ of the World?" Spinks won Olympic gold as World Light Heavyweight Champion and won the Heavyweight Championship in a massive upset against Muhammad Ali in February, and his main trainer was the same man who'd trained Ernie, so when Spinks became champ, Ernie called his old trainer to see if Leon would fight an exhibition in Chicago. I was fucking elated and agreed. The exhibition fight was set for the end of June at the International Amphitheatre, and Leon already had a rematch against Ali secured for the last week of September that year with a $4 million guarantee.

At the Woodlawn Boys Club, Kid Casey, an old-timer who was once a fighter, had the job of keeping time for everyone working out in the gym. The problem was that Kid had a tendency to cat nap during the three-minute rounds. Once the time seemed much longer than three minutes, someone in the gym would shout, "Kid!" and, on auto pilot, he would wake and yell "Time!" When I was training for the fight with Spinks, Kid came to me and asked if he could work my corner that night.

"Of course, you can," I told him, "I'll get you a shirt and a jacket just like the rest of my corner men." We had shirts and jackets made up with letters that read: Leon Spinks VS. George Mostardini for the event. Kid had a grin from ear to ear, he was so happy. Kid was a good guy who deserved to be there, and it was the least I could do.

The week of the fight was great for me. Both of us were going to have a live interview with Johnny Morris, the old receiver from the 1963 Chicago Bears championship team, who now did the sports on Channel 2 at 10 p.m. weekdays, so this was a big deal for me. I was at the studio with DeeDee and Ernie on Wednesday evening at 8:30, ready and waiting and nervous as a cat. But the time was getting close to 10, and there was still no Leon. He had a reputation for being late to everything, so everybody was getting worried. Not five minutes before the segment, he walks in. Thank God for everyone involved. After the interview Leon asked me how I got to the studio. I told him my car was parked in a lot about two blocks away. "Jump in," he said. "We'll give you a ride." Here I was in this big, black limo with Leon and his bodyguard in the front with the driver. We had some small talk, and he dropped me off at my car. *Damn,* I think, *I'm impressed. Look at the life this guy has, no work tomorrow, heading out for a drink or two for all I know.*

I didn't have a clue how an exhibition worked, so I was training like it was a championship fight. Friday morning comes, and we have the weigh-ins, which in those days were the same day as the fight. (Now the weigh-ins are the day before so fighters can get rehydrated.) Then there was nothing left to do but wait for that night. The Amphitheatre was jammed full, and lots of guys took buses from Hoagies on North Ave., Frank Morelli's bar on Armitage, and the Cuddy Club in Norridge, so 95% of the guys were already drunk by the time they got to the Amphitheatre.

The preliminary fights are done, and Leon and I are up next. First thing, Leon says to me, "You know, this is just a five-round exhibition, so we're just going to spar around the ring. Nobody's getting hurt." If that's how it goes, that's how it goes. I get into the ring, and the announcer introduces me first. The crowd of mostly Italians goes wild for me. Next, Leon comes in the ring with his championship belt on and I hear boos from the crowd. There's nothing I can do, but I feel bad for Leon because everyone in the crowd really has no idea what it takes to become the champ. He already has that $4 million guarantee in just three short months, so he doesn't even have to do this exhibition. All in all, though, Leon is a good sport about it.

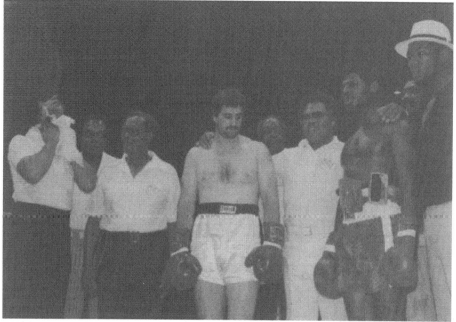

The bell rings for Round One. For the first twenty seconds, we're sparring around until—Boom!—a right upper cut hit me square on the nose, and there was no doubt in my mind that my nose is broken. Blood is pouring out of both nostrils. This, just after he tells me that nobody gets hurt. *You lousy S.O.B. Take it easy, huh?* So he had the upper hand in this round, but no problem. We still have four rounds to go. The bell rings for Round Two, and I am ready to fight. Forget that sparring bullshit. I really start to press him against the ropes and I pound him to the body with everything I've got. Already his breathing is much more labored. I land a left hook and a straight right hand, clean as a whistle, and I can see it hurts him so I definitely take that round. Back in my corner, DeeDee tells me to keep going to the body. Leon is not in the best of shape. "I knew you were going to make a war out of this as soon as he broke your nose," he says.

It's Round Three, and all my fans are going wild. They all love this, when two guys are trying to kill each other. We both fight hard in that round, back and forth, toe to toe. It's a very close round, but he probably won, mostly because of the blood pouring out of my nose like a broken faucet. In the fourth round, he starts to tire easily, and I keep pounding to the body. I know I'm hurting him because he's constantly trying to clinch. This was, without a doubt, my best round. I land a left hook that knocks the sweat off of his head into the first row and start to wonder what would happen if, by some chance, I knocked him down, or even out.

There's a lot of yelling in his corner between rounds; when the bell rings for Round Five, we pound each other until, all of a sudden, out of the corner of my eye, I see the stool from his corner go flying into the seats. Several fights seem to break out, and most of the fans in that area seem to be trying to get to someone in Leon's corner. About halfway through the last round, chairs and cups and all sorts of things start flying into the ring, and the referee stops the fight, worried about the champion's safety. People from the seats are trying to get into the ring. Turns out that the guy who threw the stool was Leon's bodyguard, a man who called himself Mr. T. He won some Best Bouncer contest downtown on Rush St. and claimed to be some kind of badass. Somebody from the crowd said something to him, and he threw the corner stool into the crowd, stirring the fans into a frenzy.

Spinks's people were worried he would get hurt and wouldn't be able to fight Ali in September, so someone suggested that he just go into the

29

locker room with me and my people for his safety. We didn't object. Temporarily safe in my dressing room, Leon and I started talking a little about the fight. My nose was badly broken and still bleeding, and DeeDee was thinking about calling off the fight I had scheduled in Detroit three weeks later. We could hear the noise from the crowd still fighting outside the door. Where else can a fight break out but at a boxing match? Everybody's a badass once they see some blood and two guys trying to pound each other senseless.

I went to take a shower, and in walked a six-foot-tall black guy with a Mohawk haircut and about forty pounds of gold chains hanging around his neck. With great urgency, he said, "Hey, you got to help us get out of this arena, we got our limo here."

I replied, "Who the fuck are you?"

"I'm Mr. T, the champ's bodyguard."

"You're the guy who threw the stool into the crowd." He admitted it, saying that they called me a so and so "Look, T., You started this whole mess, you're going to have to figure out how to fix it. Look at my nose! Do you really think I give a shit about you?!" Later on I found out that Spinks and his people almost had their limo tipped over by all the drunken, crazed, pissed-off fans.

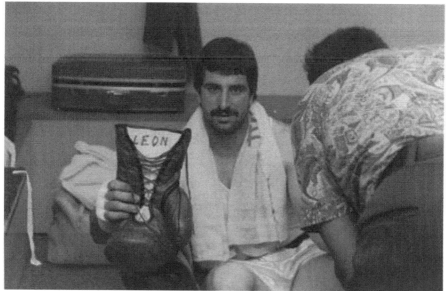

So this was my night of glory, fighting the Heavyweight Champ of the World and giving him a run for his money. I was proud of how I did!

People still see me and tell me I was kicking the shit out of him. Who knows what would have happened if the fight went the whole five rounds. I always feel good when I think about this night, not only fighting the Champ but also, this infamous Mr. T., who I thought was going to break out in tears out of fear. Mr. T. went on to have a short but successful career in some movies and a T.V. show, mostly playing that badass again. I'll bet he wishes he never came into the shower that night, because I know what he really is.

Chapter Five

That fall, I was scheduled to fight Earl McLeay at the Chicago Amphitheatre, and I was named Prospect of the Month in *The Ring Magazine* just a month earlier. McLeay was about 6 foot, 210 lbs. and I was 6'1", 213 lbs., so we were evenly matched.

The first round starts off pretty well as I press him back with my jab and a couple of body shots, but I immediately notice all the Ben-Gay or liniment he has on. In our first clinch, he tries to rub his shoulder on my face, hoping to get some in my eyes, but the referee sees what he's doing and breaks us up. Even the ref smells the mass amount of liniment he has on and tells McLeay's corner men to wipe him down, twice. The clock stops for this, over a minute, and it takes some of the momentum out of me; I had him going, and now the little edge I had is gone. When we resume fighting, there are only about forty seconds left in the round, and I don't smell a thing on him.

We both start the second round out throwing jabs at each other, and boom, he hits me with a right hand flush on the chin, and I go down, but I get up before the ref even starts his count with a big grin on my face. At least, according to DeeDee and the next morning's newscast. From the time I got hit with that punch until they stopped the fight in the sixth round, I don't remember a damn thing.

I must have fought on pure instinct. DeeDee told me I was losing the fight from then on but still did pretty well and could answer every question he asked me. "If I had any idea how bad you really felt," he told me later, "I would have stopped the fight immediately." I forfeited the bout early because McLeay had me in a corner, bombing me with punches, and when I came back to my corner, I asked where the stool was. That's when DeeDee knew how badly I was hurt and told the ref to stop. "You had that glazed look in your eyes," DeeDee told me. "You mean you fought all that time without knowing what was going on?" I guess so. It was my first loss and the only time in seventy pro and amateur fights that I got knocked down, even counting the five rounds each I went with both Leon Spinks and Ernie. Even though I was up before the ref started counting, I was still pissed about tasting that canvas.

DeeDee called the doctor into my dressing room to take a look at me. He looked in my eyes, ears, throat, nose, and then he asked me a half dozen questions, which I somehow answered correctly. He determined I had a severe concussion and said I should go to the hospital. I had also been having a lot of trouble with my nose; in training, while sparring, the slightest tap on the nose caused it to bleed profusely since Leon Spinks broke it a couple of months earlier. My nose had bled badly during the previous two fights, but tonight—not a drop. Besides the obvious concussion, the doctor said my nose was badly broken and was only getting about fifty percent air through the left nostril while the right side was closed shut. DeeDee rode home with Ernie that night instead of with me, and Kip said he'd take me to the hospital.

On the way to the Resurrection Hospital, which was close to home, I told Kip pull over, opened the door, threw up, and then did the same thing a few blocks further down. While I stood outside the car, I saw a cooler in Kip's back seat. He didn't want to tell me what was inside, so I took a look and saw he had about fifteen beers on ice. I grabbed one for me and one for him, but he said, "George, please don't drink that, let me take you to the hospital."

"A little home town cure," I responded. "My head hurts so much— how bad could a few beers be?" Despite Kip's pleas, I chugged the beer,

33

then another and another. Kip was begging me to stop all the while. I grabbed a fourth beer and told him to take me home because I felt better now (although it was probably the amount of time that had passed that made me feel better, certainly not the beer). Kip thought I was bullshitting him but I wasn't. The fight had been over for two and a half to three hours by now, and it seemed as if my memory was coming back, so he took me home and filled Ellen in. I told her I was okay, and she said, "Well, don't get pissed off at me if I keep waking you up tonight to make sure. I don't want anything to happen to you." After final pleas from Kip to go to the hospital, he left, and Ellen kept asking me how I felt. I really *did* feel better, I just didn't remember anything from that punch through the rest of the night, even to this day.

I've had minor concussions before. When you get hit with a solid shot, it's not like the cartoons, where you see birds or stars circling your head—no, you see white spots covering your vision, and you try to clinch, hold on for life, and hope they go away. But I'd always recovered (except for a headache, which eventually went away) and go back to the gym to prepare for the next fight. But this—this scary feeling when you get the shit beat out of you, throw up twice, can't remember any of it, and have to rely on your friends and the news to fill in the blanks—I wasn't used to.

My nose continued to be a problem and bled constantly while sparring, and I finally had surgery on it, which was another nightmare. Trying to sleep with packing in my nose for three days was uncomfortable, but I got through it, ready to get back in the ring. Everyone who loved me told me to quit boxing, but I just couldn't. I won my next fight less than three months later and put Earl McLeay behind me, and a month later I fought and won again. The feeling of defeat was over until the next summer when I fought Jimmy Cross.

Chapter Six

Ernie Terrell was really the only fight promoter in Chicago and had a monopoly on the fight game here for about three and a half years. Then in 1980, a new Latino promoter, Rene Rabiela, was trying to work his way in, thinking he could bring a lot of Latino fighters to Chicago and compete with Ernie in the fight game.

Many great Latino fighters who, at one time or another, held title belts were at fly weight (112 lbs.), bantam weight (118 lbs.), or featherweight (126 lbs.), and they always had a reputation for fighting savage wars. Rabicla figured he could capitalize on this. I fought for him twice, once in March of '79, when I won an easy third-round knockout over Gene Abbott from Cincinnati. It was a co-main event fight, and one of the fighters on the card was the great Rubén Olivares, who held belts for both bantam and featherweight divisions for many years. Olivares had over a hundred fights, was a two-time champ, and was idolized in Mexico, so the promoter knew he could bring in tons of money. The second fight took place in March 1980 as the main event: ten rounds against Alfredo "Mongol" Ortiz, Heavyweight Champion of Mexico. He'd even fought some eight to ten times in Europe, where he had a reputation for his durability. He fought the best fighters and had never been KO'd in his career.

I knew this fight was going to be a tough one not only because he was a warhorse but also because it was going to be a mostly Latino audience, which would certainly be cheering for Mongol, their champion. Crowd reaction can have a huge impact on judges. Fans booing and rooting against you sends negative vibes to the judges, while a cheering, loving crowd can sway point decisions, and if the crowd cheers when you get hit but not when your opponent gets hit, the judges think the fighter with the cheers may be winning. I knew I had my hands full, and this fight would probably go the whole ten rounds.

I trained especially hard for the fight with Mongol. Every morning before work, I ran eight miles and did some exercises, and after work I hit the gym to train and spar. DeeDee worked with me a lot on movement, going side to side. He'd seen Mongol fight a couple years earlier and saw he didn't do a lot of dancing around but mostly stood in one spot, brawled, and came straight at his opponents. DeeDee taught me how to focus more on moving side to side to stay out of Mongol's way and still be able to catch him with hooks to the body. Come fight time, I was in great shape and felt confident. Mongol was ranked 9th at the time, so a win could get me in the Top 10.

Before the fight, Channel 2 sports anchor Tim Weigel wanted to do an interview with me at Hoagies Pub, where I often went after Chicago fights. Hoagies was owned by the Spilotro Brothers, and every Chicagoan in the '70s and '80s knows what happened to them (the Santoro Brothers in Martin Scorcese's *Casino* are even based on Tony and Michael Spilotro). The interview was great publicity for Hoagies, and Michael Spilotro never forgot that and treated me well from the start. Many bus trips to the fights were organized from Hoagies; fans would come before the fight to eat and drink, take the bus to the fight, and come right back after to eat and drink some more. Ever since my fight with Bolden, I never paid for anything and Michael would treat my father, sister, and me to dinner and drinks each and every time we came. At the time, I had no idea Michael was involved with the Chicago Outfit—his brother Tony ran Las Vegas while Michael ran Hoagies—but it wouldn't have mattered to me because he always treated me like a gentleman. Tim Weigel was a big boxing fan and loved coming to my fights, and I respected that he was also very fair in what he reported. I had some friends of mine at the table with me for the interview with him, and everyone enjoyed a beer except for me because I was in training. I tried staying humble, not wanting to get ahead of myself, and everyone had a good time, including Michael Spilotro—overall a great night leading up the fight.

It was the end of March, so fight night was chilly. It was held at the Uptown Theatre, right down the street from the Aragon Ballroom where I had a dozen fights before. The Uptown was, frankly, a cold and dirty dump. The dressing room could only fit two people at once, so people had to rotate coming in and out, and it was so cold that we all had our jackets on during the preliminary fights. As I was waiting, I started to wonder to myself why I even took this fight. While DeeDee wrapped my hands, I could see by his expression that he didn't like the place either. But working up the ladder means you don't get to fight in the greatest of places. We were happy to be called to the ring just so we could be moving.

After we all entered the ring, the MC led the fans in singing both the American and Mexican national anthems, and the crowd went wild after the Mexican anthem. Not a good sign for me.

The referee introduces us and we touch gloves, then the bell rings for Round One and we finally get down to business. Mongol sticks out his left hand and we touch gloves again, a sign of good sportsmanship before going to war to show there's nothing personal, just business. Now, we battle. Halfway through the round, we end up in a corner firing bombs at each other for about forty-five seconds. We both land our best punches, and I connect and connect again, but he doesn't move. Now I know his durability. Then Mongol lands a punch that nearly knocks my bottom teeth right through my skin, putting a nickel-sized hole just below my bottom lip. The first round ends and I'm in my corner. DeeDee says, "When he gets in real close, use the right uppercut, left hook to the head, and then back to the body."

In Round Two, I start using my jab. Mongol wasn't very fast, so I know he wants to get into a slug fest and really brawl, but I think I can outbox him. The taste of copper runs down my throat from the cut in my mouth, and I still have nine rounds to go. Mongol takes three solid jabs to close in for a brawl, so I take DeeDee's advice and nail him with a right uppercut, left hook, and a left hook to the body. Each punch connects, and

37

the same combo works over and over. Sometimes I follow with a right to the body and another right uppercut. He's a tough guy, but I can tell I'm wearing him down.

After about the sixth round, DeeDee says, "You can take this guy out. Go for it!" When things are going your way in a fight, you hate to change things up, but DeeDee has never let me down, so I listen. The bell rings for Round Seven, and I go in for the kill. But really, I just start to brawl and stop boxing. This is just what Mongol wants; he's been looking for me to leave myself open so he can land his best shots, and he wins the round because I'm reckless in my approach. One punch can turn an entire fight around. Between rounds DeeDee reminds me, "Don't forget all we worked on. I didn't tell you to be stupid, you know he punches back pretty good himself. Go back in and do what you were doing."

At the start of the eighth round, I can tell Mongol blew his wad in the seventh. I use the jab and combinations and give him a good beating in the eighth and ninth rounds. I wonder to myself, *What's keeping this guy up?* Mongol has the heart of a lion and just refuses to give up. I have that taste of copper now more than before. When I spit in the bucket, it's all blood. There is only one round to go, and I know I can finish him easily. Three minutes is a lifetime in boxing. Just punching a heavy bag for three minutes is exhausting—now imagine that bag punching back for nine rounds while you've been sucking down your own blood. I just hope Mongol doesn't get a second wind.

The bell rings for Round Ten, and I give him a good beating again. Mongol's tired and out of gas. I have more stamina but still need to be cautious. Mongol needed to save his reputation, and he wasn't going to be knocked out. Suddenly the bell rings, and the fight is over. We shake hands and wait for the decision, but I think we both know I have won. The judges announce a unanimous decision for me.

After the decision, Mongol and I headed back to our locker rooms, and I felt that same great sense of relief. I'll get some time off from training to spend with my family for a few days before going back to train for my next opponent. I started to take a shower, but there was no hot water so I decided to wait. As I got dressed, though, I heard the water running in the shower. Out of curiosity, I went to see who would be brave enough to take an ice cold shower. It's Mongol Ortiz, sitting on a folding chair, still in his trunks and boxing shoes and his hands still wrapped, letting the ice cold water run over him. I said, "Mongol, you've got a lot of balls to sit in there." He said something to me in Spanish with a smile on his face, and that's the last time I ever saw him.

I finished getting dressed so I can get paid and get the hell out of there. DeeDee and I found Rabiela talking with my manager, he hands my manager a check for $600, to be split between him and DeeDee, naturally I said, "Where's mine?"

Rabiela reached into his pocket and pulled out a wad of cash from the gate, the money paid by the fans to get in, and said, "I got yours."

Because the main event was the last fight and all the other fighters had already been paid, there wasn't enough left over for me. "I was supposed to be paid $1,500," I reminded him.

"That's gotta be at least $1,250, count it."

By now I was getting angry. "If you think I'm going to lay this mess on a table and count it in front of everyone walking out, you're nuts."

Rabiela said, "It's all I've got except for some change," and he pulls out the inside of his pockets. "Do you want that?"

I knew from my last experience with him that a check would bounce, and we'd agreed on cash. So in the car going home, I counted the mess of twenties, fives, and singles adding up to $1,252. This was my big take for fighting ten rounds with the 9th ranked fighter in 1980—$1,252. All the training, the fight, the hole in my mouth that I stuck a napkin into, for a lousy $1,252.

Don't misunderstand, I'm still a happy man. I did what I had to do, and I won the fight with minimal damage to myself. Not all fights end like this one, and promoters don't usually pay with money from the gate. Things didn't work out like he thought, and Rabiela took a bath on this fight, which was his last in Chicago. Putting on a fight costs a lot of money: bringing in the fighters, putting them up in a hotel, feeding them, paying for their taxis to and from the venue, not to mention paying them for the fight itself. Rabiela brought in all those Latino fighters, tried to compete with Terrell, and lost his shirt.

After the fight, we head to Hoagies for some beer and pizza and laughed about the whole ordeal. I took the napkin out of my mouth, grabbed a bottle of Miller Lite, chugged about three quarters of it down and felt a whole lot better. I wolfed down the rest, ordered another and tried to organize my money from the fight. *It's all good, it is what it is*. A good win for me, a lot of laughs, a few bucks, and a real good experience.

Chapter Seven

To me boxing is not a sport—it's a crude *damnatio ad bestias*, a legal way for two human beings to try to kill each other. It's really the only way you can commit a homicide and not get charged. It's a way for the managers, promoters, and hangers on to make money off your blood.

At the time of this fight, I was ranked #10 and my opponent, Floyd "Jumbo" Cummings was #9. He had never lost a fight or even gone to a decision. He was undefeated, 18:0, and he won every bout by KOs, and I mean knock OUTs. He knocked everyone out cold. Still, Jumbo was genuinely a down-to-earth person afterward. Everyone makes mistakes, and he paid for his with eight years in Joliet prison, where he put the boxing program to good use. He grew up in prison and was about 6"2" and over 220 pounds of solid rock.

The fight was in the summer of 1980, just when ESPN started broadcasting weekly fights. Terrell snagged a spot on ESPN for me, which would be my fifth out of seven fights on ESPN. I had already fought four times on the station earlier in the year, and six weeks prior I had fought and won a fifth-round KO, but I hurt my left elbow so bad I couldn't even spar. Still, there were two reasons I couldn't cancel the fight. First, Jumbo had a big reputation as a badass for his past. How would it look if I canceled? My manhood was at stake. I always said it's better to get beaten up than walk away from a fight. You are the one who has to look in the mirror every day. You're the one people will talk about. Really, you should never care or make decisions based on what anyone thinks of you, but deep down everyone does so anyway.

I probably shouldn't have taken this fight, not because Jumbo was undefeated but because my elbows hurt so much I couldn't even straighten them. But the money was big for me, and I couldn't pass it up. That's what will suck a fighter into the ring any day, the money. The who, where, and when don't matter; *how much* am I going to make, that's the bottom line. I didn't even think about my injuries. I smelled one of the biggest paydays to date and accepted.

Strategy was flying through my head leading up to the fights. I needed to figure out a way to get one of those long shot bombs in there, preferably early in the fight. Maybe try and catch him while it's early and he's still nervous (every fighter who has ever stepped in the ring before thousands of people and knows how many more watching on ESPN is nervous. Everyone, even the best of the best). I know *I* can go ten rounds, but can *he*? The furthest he has ever been is one minute into the fifth round. If I can't catch him early, maybe I can outlast him. He was a big weightlifter, and boxing and weightlifting don't mix well. It makes the body too tight and uses up a lot of energy. In boxing, being loose and relaxed will let you fight forever. So that's my plan since I know for sure my elbows won't last long, and I'll have to rely on my shoulders to push off when we're in close in the clinches.

At this time I didn't even have a manager, only DeeDee. Every day he told me to cancel the fight, saying, "What the hell do you care what people think or say?" The pain agreed with him, but I wanted the payday. He just shook his head and told me I was fighting for the wrong reason. Again, I knew he was right, but it was too late to back out.

It's fight day. ESPN would give the fighters a pair of trunks and a robe with their logo for advertising, which I never liked. I had a pair of white trunks with a thick black stripe down the sides that I always wore and considered my lucky trunks. DeeDee and I have to recruit two guys who always work the corner with DeeDee for out-of-town fights because I have no one else with me anymore. I say to myself, *A hometown boy using unknowns in his corner. You lose a couple of fights, and everyone goes away. I've seen this with other fighters. Now it's me who's the chump. No corner men, bad elbows, and a tough opponent. This could make for a very long night.*

At weigh-in, my opponent is 224 and I'm 212. We shake hands and wish each other luck.

It's Round One and he comes straight at me. I had seen him fight before, so I knew he would do this, he was always looking for a knockout. I rolled with a couple of punches and saw an opening for a good left jab. I threw it and it landed, but just as I expected , my left elbow hyperextended and serious pain shot through my elbow. I knew it, I tried to deny it, but there it was, and now I was in trouble. Whenever you're in a ring with someone—an undefeated fighter with all KOs no less—and you're hurt, you are, plain and simple, fucked. All I can do is try and disguise my injury the best I can, but I know it's gonna be a long night. I pull away from the clinch and feel the pain in my right elbow, it's not as bad as the left but bad enough. All these thoughts are running through my head. I should have listened to everyone and not taken this fight. But…the money. I need to concentrate and not lose my focus.

The first round ends and DeeDee tells me, "Your elbows are shot."

"How do you know that already?" I asked.

"I can see how you're fighting. I can see the expression on your face." DeeDee is worried because he knows I can't punch, and so do the guys in my opponents corner. "It's too late now. Maybe, when he comes in close, you can throw some uppercuts."

I take his advice at the start of the second round and start to do a little better, but every punch, every combination starts off with a jab, and I have none. After the fourth round, DeeDee pleads with me to stop the fight and plainly tells me, "You're getting the shit beat out of you."

I replied, "Never, let it play out. Maybe he'll get tired of pounding on me or have a heart attack or something. I am not going to quit." DeeDee laughed about the heart attack and said he would respect my call, for now.

The fifth and sixth rounds were pretty much the same shit, but towards the end of the sixth, I catch him coming in with a right uppercut and left hook that stagger him. I chase him and land some more good shots. It's my best round in a long time and he's also slowing down. So maybe, just maybe, I can turn this thing around. But now–just what I needed–I'm dealing with another problem. My left eye is swelling shut from all the punishment I am taking.

The start of the seventh round, I know I need to do something drastic. I don't know if my body can come through for me. I land some punches, he lands some. I see openings and try and take them, but my elbows fail me. All I can think is *why didn't I wait until they were better, until I saw a doctor? Why did I jump at the money so fast, like an idiot? Everything I have ever worked for is going down the drain because of my greed.* All these doubts are running through my head a hundred miles an hour, but it's too late. *You knew something like this was going to happen. You let it happen.*

It's the first minute of the ninth round, and my eye is closed tight. The referee takes me to see the doctor, who says I can no longer see out of my left eye and stops the fight. Relief goes through me, but I wish I could have finished the last round and a half. My opponent wins by a Technical Knockout due to my injury. I look over at Jumbo's corner and see them jumping up and down with happiness. I look over at my corner and see the agony of defeat. I have no manager, no real corner men, and I can't even defend myself right. Just like with Jimmy Cross, the fight goes on the books as a TKO loss, even though I was never even *near* being knocked down or out. What the hell was I thinking?

DeeDee and I went to Ernie to get my money, and I stared at the check a long time. Even though this was my biggest payday, it wasn't enough for what I went through. No fucking way. Not then, and not now.

It was about eleven o'clock, and I gave DeeDee a ride home to 72nd and Cottage Grove. There was a small neighborhood tavern right below his apartment, and he offered to buy me a drink. All I wanted to do was to go home and crawl into a hole, but I knew DeeDee had something on his mind. I agree to one drink, and when we go in I'm the only white guy in the place, but they knew who I was and that DeeDee was my trainer. The bar had shown the fight on TV, so I had a lot of armchair quarterbacks telling me what I should have done. We sat at the bar, ordered a drink, and DeeDee started to talk.

"Don't let this ruin your career," DeeDee tells me, "and don't let this ruin your life. Don't let this linger in your head. Your head is your most powerful muscle; it controls the rest of you. We both know why you didn't

44

cancel the fight, why you even took it in the first place. You knew best what the outcome was going to be. If you don't want to tell anyone that's fine, I won't tell anyone either. Rest up, I'll talk to Ernie, and we will fight another day. Don't let this destroy you."

I thanked DeeDee for his support, had a few more drinks, gave him a big hug, and got in my car to leave. All the way home, I thought about how I had cheated myself and everyone who cared about me. There was no way to ever redeem myself from this. I never told anyone because I was, still am, truly embarrassed. This fight, the Jimmy Cross fight, and many others have stayed with me my whole damn life. They've made me depressed and oftentimes even sick to my stomach.

I was 99.5% sure I would lose. Anytime I was asked about the fight, I just said he was the better man that night. I didn't make excuses or blame the loss on anyone or anything but myself. It's a long, long time to hold on to something inside you. My elbows healed, but I hated myself after that fight and never really recovered from it.

I never thought too hard about all the stuff that was to come afterwards, only the paycheck. Jumbo went to New York and, about two months later, lost a ten-rounder to Renaldo Snipes. That *could have been me*, I thought, *had I used my head*. Then Snipes got a title shot at Larry Holmes a couple of years later and made a lot more money than I ever did, even though he lost. Seems the hard way is the only way anything ever stuck in my head.

The loss of a fight stays with you a long, *long* time. Every time you're alone. Every time you look in the mirror, it enters your mind. *Enjoy the money while you can, it's all you have left. You sure as hell don't have any pride.* And you feel sick to your stomach. Your worst opponent is the one you see every day, the one you look at every morning, yourself.

Chapter Eight

September 1980 at the International Amphitheatre was a big night for me. Cable television had started a whole new trend for boxing, and I was fighting the main event on Ernie's ESPN card for the third straight month. I fought and won two bouts by KO in July and August, but this fight was against Amos Haynes, whose record was 15:4 at the time. Tall and lanky, at about 6'3" and 203 lbs., Haynes actually looked like a football wide receiver. I could see he was in excellent shape and knew I would have my hands full, but I was also in great shape, too, and could go ten rounds without much of a problem.

When we got to the Amphitheatre that night, ESPN had their cameras set up and the place was packed, but one face by the cameras stood out. It was Duane Bobick, great Olympic boxer, who now was an announcer for ESPN. Haynes and I had a brief interview with Bobick before fighting the main event. Haynes didn't say much to me except that he was going to knock me out; I just laughed and said, "You'll be the one picking yourself up off the floor pretty soon."

We entered the ring, got our instructions, and went to our corners. DeeDee Armor told me whack him to the body. "He can't have a 30 inch waist; I think you'll hurt him. He is going to use that jab, so keep your chin tucked down. You look stronger, so force the fight."

The bell rings for Round One, and Haynes stands tall, trying to use his height and jab on me, but it's not very hard because he has his weight on his back foot. Great for me—I come forward throwing my own jab, even though it's a little short. Then I throw a right-left, right-left to the body and he clinches. Towards the end of the round, I throw two to the body, come up and throw a right then a left. They don't all connect, but I'm forcing the fight. The bell rings, round's over, and Haynes nails me with a left hook. He gets a warning from the referee but pretends it was an accident. The second round goes the same way almost to a tee, even the left hook after the bell. Now I know the prick did it on purpose. *I can play this game, too.*

In the third round, I corner him and position myself to the left of the ref, and I let a left go real hard, real low. I continue to fight while he's complaining to the ref, and I clinch at the bell so he can't hit again. He walks to his corner still complaining to the ref, but to no avail. DeeDee smiles at me and says to keep it going. All three rounds are mine. The fourth starts, and after about a minute, he hits me with a left hook and cuts me below my right eye. I had a small cut under my eye during training but this punch opened it up pretty good. I see a big smile on his face. *What an asshole! He's nuts if he thinks he's going to win because of this small cut.* DeeDee will stop the bleeding between rounds, and it was below my eye, so no blood was going in my eye. Right before the bell, he hits me low. The ref sees it and he takes a point away.

Back in my corner, DeeDee says the cut is just a scratch and not to worry about it. "This round, I want to see you take this guy out. Not the seventh, eighth, or ninth, *this round*. This guy is nuts and he wants a street fight." He laughs and says, "I know you tell me all the time how you were the king of street fighting at the park where you hung out at when you were a kid. But this is serious, this guy is a real dirty fighter. So put him on his ass, and let's get the fuck out of here."

The bell rings for Round Five, and I go after Haynes with his own tactics. I use my shoulder to corner him. He wants to use the middle of the ring, but I won't let him out. Halfway through the round, I throw a left uppercut about a foot low and catch him right on the bottom of his protective cup. There are low punches, and there are *low* punches. They will *numb your balls*. I know what I'm doing, I'm tired of his dirty shit. I hit him and hear him start whining. I know it hurts, but the ref never sees me do it. While Haynes looks to the ref for help, I bomb him with about a half dozen solid shots to the head, and he crumbles, down and out.

He took the ten count, and I won a fifth-round KO over the dirtiest fighter I have ever fought. After he woke up, he pleaded with the ref to no avail and was pissed. Right away, I told DeeDee to take off my gloves in case this guy tried anything. DeeDee laughed and said, 'I guess you want to show me your great street fighting."

"You never know with a guy like this," I said.

DeeDee then points out that Haynes' corner men are holding him up from falling on his face. "He's not doing any more fighting tonight," he laughed. "Come on, they want you to say something on ESPN."

Bobick showed me some of the fight they had on tape, and I explained my strategy for the people watching the fight. After that was over, I changed clothes and went with DeeDee to get paid then to the doctor about the cut under my eye. Thankfully, I didn't even need stitches, the doctor put three butterfly bandages on it and we were on our way. I took DeeDee home and, like always, we stopped in the tavern. We pounded down some Crown Royal and laughed about how dirty the fight was. "I do know one thing," I said. "His balls are the size of grapefruits right now. That punch hurt him so bad he was squealing."

DeeDee said "Screw him, he got exactly what he deserved," and I totally agreed.

Chapter Nine

In February 1981, Ernie set up a fight for me against an opponent that I will not name just to give him credit for his "victory." The fight was ten rounds in White Plains, New York, and was going to be on ESPN, so it was good money for me.

I flew to New York with DeeDee, and when we landed, a van took us to the New York Boxing Commission for my physical to fight. A doctor looked me over completely, took a urine test, checked my blood pressure, my nose, and the cuts over my eye, and gave me a brain scan; I was cleared to fight, and they took $25 for a New York boxing license. After the flight and a two and a half hour physical, DeeDee and I were starving. The commission took us back to the hotel where we checked in and immediately went to the restaurant. No drinks for me, but DeeDee had his usual couple shots of Crown Royal whisky. The next afternoon around 4:30, the van picked us up again and took us to the arena.

It was beautiful there, a little more high class than what I was used to. After we got in the dressing room, we got a look at who I would be fighting. He looked about the same height and weight as me, but DeeDee noticed something on his left hand: his third knuckle was badly swollen and went halfway up his hand. DeeDee told me that he hurt his hand recently, which could be a big break. He decided to watch my opponent get his hands wrapped and signed by the commissioner to make sure there was no funny business, and when he came over to do mine, DeeDee told me he saw the opponent wince when they wrapped his left hand. "Put that in your memory bank," he told me.

When we entered the ring and we were getting our instructions from the referee, I could see the guy was probably two inches taller than I was but the weight was the same. The crowd cheered loud for their hometown man because he was 16:0 with 13 KO's; however, he'd never gone more than six rounds, and now he had a bad hand.

The bell rings for the first round. Here we go. He uses his left hand as a range finder, just sticking it out there and trying to fire a straight right. I can see he's trying to pop me with his right and avoid him. Halfway through the round, I get a perfect opportunity and fire a brutal left hook. It lands right on the button (on the point of his chin), and down he goes, right on the seat of his pants. This is the first time he's ever been knocked down. (Most one-punch KO's are right on the button.) So now I've nailed him and he's hurt. It seems like the referee keeps pushing me back to give him more time to recover, and when he does get up he clinches me hard. He's pretty strong and I'm trying to get out when he tries to lay out the left, but I throw an overhand right that drops him again. When he gets up again, the round is over. Back in my corner, DeeDee tells me to keep firing and remember his left hand. At the start of the second round, the last thing he wants to do is fight—he wants to run, so he basically gives me the round. Same with the third and fourth rounds. When a fighter has never been hurt and gets nailed like this, all that bravado starts to leave and he goes into survival mode.

He starts to fight better in the fifth, sixth, and seventh rounds; they're all pretty even and could go either way. The eighth round is his best: he catches me with a straight right and cuts my left eyebrow. Between rounds, DeeDee tells me not to worry about the cut and to go after this guy hard because he's very tired. The ninth starts, and I go after him hard, cornering him. He tries to clinch, but I use my free hand to pound away at him. Towards the end of the round, I see he is dead tired. He's even dropping it after he throws it, so I take advantage and fire a left hook over his right hand. Well, the left hook wasn't the greatest, but it was good enough to put him on the seat of his pants again, the third time this fight.

51

He is up before the bell, though, so we go to our corners before the tenth and final round.

One of DeeDee's tricks of the trade was to mix crushed up asthma pills in the water, so three to four big gulps would open up my lungs and I could fight for what seemed like forever. In between gulps, he tells me "Knock this asshole out, he's ready to go." Before the bell rings for the final round I feel anxious and fidgety. I tell myself to relax or else I might make a costly mistake. The bell rings for the final round, and we have to touch gloves again before the last round. I guess it's a long tradition of sportsmanship—what a joke! All I want to do is put this prick in the hospital. We go at it, and he is a master clincher. I try to get the referee's attention and yell, "Why don't you break this up?" but he pretends to not hear me. I hold him off as long as I can until the bell rings and the fight is over. I have never been more confident that I've won a fight.

We wait for the decision now, but it's taking too long. I tell DeeDee, "These motherfuckers are going to steal this from me."

"They can't, it's too obvious you won." Finally, they announce a majority decision. I know this is bullshit right away.

Now in New York, bouts are scored round by round, so no matter the number of knockdowns, you can only win or lose the round. The first judge announces 7-2-1 for me—good but I know what's coming. The other two judges go 5-5 even, so it's a majority draw. I feel like I swallowed my throat. The fans go into a frenzy, knowing I won the fight, and start booing, throwing cups, and chanting "Fix, fix, fix."

What bullshit.

DeeDee spat at the referee, who didn't have a single thing to say. Talk about getting it stuck in your ass. DeeDee and I go to the dressing room and start destroying anything within reach. Next thing we know, the doctor came in to put six or seven stitches over my left eye. The promoter came in after and apologized for the outcome. A lot of good that does us, but then he offered us an interesting proposition:

"How would you like a rematch in three and a half months?"

I scoffed, "Why? Unless I kill the guy, they'll give him the decision."

Then the promoter says the magic words: "I will double your money at least, and the fight will be twelve rounds."

DeeDee and I promised to let him know before going home tomorrow, I get dressed, and go back to the hotel. Right away we head down to the restaurant to talk business. DeeDee ordered a double shot of Crown Royal for himself and a light beer for me. My mind was spinning over how I got fucked so bad. I was shocked at the decision, but DeeDee was pissed. I'd never seen him disrespect a ref like that before, and even though we laughed a little about it, I could tell he wasn't proud of it. That's the chance you take when you fight out of town, but at least the promoter gave me a chance at redemption and financial gain.

DeeDee and I talked about it over a couple more drinks; the more we drank, the more we said we were going to ask him for, until we finally decided on a figure close to three times what I got tonight. Ernie had driven to New York because he couldn't bear the thought of flying, but he eventually joined us. Ernie went to the pay phone to call the promoter, who laughed at our demand and threw out another figure. We countered, and it went back and forth for a few minutes until we finally decided on a price. I couldn't believe it—what turned out to be a tragic night for me was now going to make me two and a half times what I just fought for. This twelve-rounder was going to have a few stipulations, including a different referee and different judges. I figured, *I have some kind of chance now. I can win this fight. Payday's gonna be huge.*

While we wolfed down steaks and drinks, the three of us talked again about how I got fucked tonight. But then we started talking about what could be. *What could be?* You think about this phrase constantly. When your eye's almost torn out and pain is shooting through every inch of your entire body—*what could be?* This is the phrase that keeps every boxer dreaming, hoping, and praying—fighting.

Chapter Ten

I took a couple of days off after we got home and started training again. I couldn't do too much too soon because I still had stitches above my eye, but by the time I got back to the gym, Ernie Terrell had the contract from New York with all of our agreed-upon conditions. We signed and sent the contract back. The rematch was set.

Once I got the stitches out, I began to train like never before. After all, this was going to be twelve rounds and I had never gone past ten. I had two perfect guys to spar with that were similar to my opponent: James "Quick" Tillis and James "Money" Lumpkins. These fighters were tall, fast, and strong, so I could practice working out of his clinches. Both guys had great left jabs and good, straight and fast right hands, so I had my hands full every day. Good fighters to spar with is essential; there's no learning otherwise. *No pain, no gain,* and all that. So I flew into my training with a deep desire to hurt my last opponent badly. I got mean and had real hate for this guy who, just a couple of months ago, I never even knew. I wanted to kill him if if I could, and I knew he felt the same way.

I ran hard every day, I worked harder at my job, and I trained as hard as I could at the gym. I laid off booze, pizza, and fried foods. I had a chip on my shoulder as big as a tree and made myself mad at everything and everybody. The thought of the money and *what could be* was in my blood. I needed to be angry and, in some ways, I even liked it. Training was intense, and my anxiety was through the roof as the day approached. I worried that either one of us could get injured and the fight would be postponed. For the money I was going to get, all I wanted was to get in that ring and do my thing.

We changed our sparring routine by going straight ten-minute stints with three different fighters. Besides Quick Tillis and Lumpkins, I had Walter Moore as a sparring partner, the resident Woodlawn Boys Club fighter whose career I ended. I was fighting thirty minutes straight with only two minutes of rest in-between to build up stamina. DeeDee, always on top of things, also reminded me that my opponent had a bad left hand and would watch them wrap his hand again. DeeDee watched me work out every minute of every training for every fight. He was genuinely concerned for his fighters.

As fight day approached, DeeDee and I took a cab to O'Hare to catch a flight to NYC. Ernie and Walter hit the road three days earlier. The same character picked us up in the van and took us to the boxing commission for another physical. New York was the only state where boxers had to take a legitimate physical, which was pretty strict but good for the fighters. Afterward, the driver took us to the hotel and, as he dropped us off, said to me, "I hope you don't get screwed like the last time." I replied, "You're not the only one."

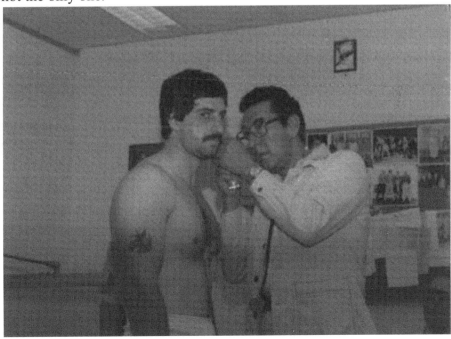

55

DeeDee and I went to dinner, talked strategy, took a walk, and then went to sleep. It was always hard to sleep the night before a fight—my mind was racing and my nerves kicked in—so after breakfast the next day, I took a couple hours for a good nap. Before I knew it, it was 4:30 and the van came to pick us up. DeeDee was still strategizing on the way to the theater, but my mind was elsewhere, racing like a thoroughbred.

We arrived, went to our dressing room, and I tried to stretch out and loosen up while DeeDee talked. Then I lay down on the training table and tried to relax. We still had about an hour or so before he would wrap my hands.

DeeDee, still talking, said, "Even if a fighter has the same talent as you, you can still outwork him, out-heart him, and out-tough him. If you work hard enough ,it doesn't matter and you know you worked hard for this fight. You have heart, desire, and toughness, so put it all together tonight, and let's go home happy. Use your heart, your guts, your stamina, because you beat him once, even if they called it a draw. This time you're in much better shape, so knock his ass out. Put that hard left hook over his hanging right hand, right on the point of his chin." He wrapped my hands a little early so he could take a peek at my opponent. He comes back and, sure enough, he's still having problems with his left hand "Keep this in mind."

Somebody yelled, "It's time!" into the dressing room, so we headed down toward the ring. I was glad as hell to just get started already.

DeeDee, Ernie, Walter, that's my team. We get into the ring and the MC announces us. The fans cheer pretty loud for me. They remember how the last fight turned out. The ref gives us our instructions and we head to our corners to wait for the bell.

The bell rings for Round One. Thank God, now it's time to go to work. He comes out pumping that jab at me, but his weight is on his back foot when he throws it, no power in it. This tells me he remembers my power from the last fight, I have a psychological edge on him. It's not much but it's something. Towards the end of the first round I wait for his jab. I remember when he throws his jab he tends to drop his right hand, so when he does I fire a left hook. It lands hard but a little high, mostly by his right eye. He immediately clinches, but the bell rings for the end of the round.

56

In my corner DeeDee tells me to follow the hook with a right then another left hook to the body. We meet in the middle of the ring for Round Two. He fires the jab at me. It glances off the side of my face, so I throw a left hook, right, left hook to the body, forcing him back. I throw a right to the body and follow with a left hook to the head. Now we're against the ropes so he clinches, but I still have my right hand free and land four hard shots to his ribs before he can really hold on. He looks worried and his right eye is swollen underneath to the size of a mouse. The round's over and DeeDee tells me to push him back hard when he tries to clinch. Try to keep one hand working. The third and fourth rounds are nearly the same, with me chasing after him. I feel that I won the first four rounds.

The fifth round begins, and he finally starts to come after me. We have a couple hard exchanges and the crowd is going wild. During the sixth round, I see a great chance after he throws his jab and I fire a left hook that hits him right on the chin, and down he goes. He gets up at the count of six, takes the eight count, and does nothing but clinch the rest of the round.

By now he has swelling above and below his eye, so DeeDee tells me between rounds to go after his right eye. He seems to fight better for the seventh and eighth rounds, but I'm still getting good hits in. Towards the end of the eighth, we have a punch-for-punch blastoff, but the bell rings and ends the round.

Back in my corner, DeeDee tells me the guy blew his wad and is dead tired. "Go after him, look for the hook." During the ninth he starts his clinching again, so I just keep pounding the body the best I can for the rest of round. In the tenth I can see his right eye is closed enough that his vision is impaired, so I start to throw jabs at his eye. Now it's jab for jab but he's still on his back foot so my jabs are harder.

After the round, I tell DeeDee I need some of his magic asthma water. I'm tired and I know we're going into never-never land, two more rounds than I've ever gone before. He gives me four good gulps. My lungs open up, and I feel better already, but DeeDee tells me it's just psychological and I should have no problem going the last two rounds.

The eleventh round starts and I immediately go after his right eye, which is almost swollen shut. When he clinches, I turn his body so the referee can't see and try and rub my thumb in his eye. We are still using the old 8oz. gloves without the thumb, so I have to be careful—if the referee sees me, he'll take away a point. Before the twelfth starts, DeeDee tells me, "You have to win this round. Don't give them the chance to steal this fight like the last time."

The bell rings for the final round. We come to the center of the ring, touch gloves, and go to work. I start firing bombs towards his right eye. It's so swollen, I know he can't see out of it. Out of the blue, he throws a left hook that catches me square on the chin. I immediately start seeing white spots all around me. My brain has just bounced against my skull. My instincts take over, and I quickly clinch; the referee breaks us up, but I clinch again. In those twenty-five or thirty seconds I can see again. I know I have to start pounding away at this guy I can't let him win the last round.

Not thirty seconds after he tags me, I land a right hand and the sheer force of the punch tangles his feet and he falls against the ropes—a knockdown. The ref gives him the eight count. *This is great*, I'm beaming, *I came back hard and won the last round big.* After the count, I get him against the ropes and throw punches for the last fifteen seconds until the bell ends the fight.

Except for a massive headache, I feel great, and I know I've won this fight. We go back to our corners and wait for the decision. DeeDee says, "Good job, you fought hard, you won this fight."

The announcer comes out with the score cards. "Let's give them both a great big hand for tonight's fight!" and the crowd stands up cheering. This never fails to makes me feel good. I gave them my heart and soul, sweat and blood for their entertainment, and they appreciate it. The announcer continues, "We have a split decision!" I look at DeeDee *No fucking way, not again.* DeeDee tells me to take it easy and hear what he has to say. "Mostardini, 8-3-1." I tense up as he announces 6-5-1 for my opponent. I look over at DeeDee I can't believe what I'm hearing. Again, 6-5-1. He knows he lost this fight and, just like the first one, and so does everyone else, including the judges—they just don't want to admit it! Not even a fucking draw. I lost.

Up until the late sixties and early seventies, fights were judged by 2 judges and the referee, who was usually a former fighter himself. He could see the action first hand, punch by punch, and could tell how hard the punches were because he would move around the ring with the fighters. Since then, though, referees were replaced by all panel judges and the ref only moderates the fights. In those days, it was typical for judges to lean toward their hometown fighter when the scoring seemed close: if the hometown favorite was still on his feet the judges might score in his favor. The judges are assigned by the state, so having the hometown favorite win means money for the state and lets the judges keep their job. Many fighters are also backed by corporations or big businesses, so they need to make sure their investment pays off. The decisions are not always fair, but it's all about the money.

I told DeeDee, "Let's get our money and get the fuck out of this place. I will never fight again. I fucking quit this primitive sport." I am so pissed I can't think straight.

"Fuck these guys," DeeDee said. "This is why I hate going out of town. They stick it *way* up there."

As we fumed in the dressing room with Ernie and Walter, the promoter came in. I ran and grabbed him by the throat, yelling "You promised it would be the square!" DeeDee, Ernie, and Walter pulled me off of him. "Take it easy!" DeeDee yelled at me. "Do you want to end up in jail?"

I apologized to the promoter, who handed me my check and said, "I'm really sorry, they want to move this guy up. I know he's not going to make it, but that's what they want." After tonight the commission knew it made a mistake, they knew this guy was never going to get to the top, but they couldn't back out. "I'm really sorry. I feel so bad, I have to make it up to you."

"That's what you said last time this happened," I said.

"I kept my word," he said. "I changed refs, the judges, gave you more than twice the pay. I am sorry, but I don't know what else to say. To make up for it, I'll let you fight this guy Frank Schramm for good money." I said I would talk it over with DeeDee and Ernie and get back to him later that night.

I took a shower, cleaned up, and took a long look at my face. My right eye was all black and blue, my forehead was scratched, bruised, and bleeding. Then it all began to sink it. I had just been robbed of this fight.

59

I screamed out loud at no one in particular. DeeDee and Ernie tried to calm me down, reminding me about all the money I made tonight with another big payday in two months. "I know how you feel, I was robbed a couple of times in my career," Ernie says. "I know it hurts badly, but don't give up this big payday and an easy fight."

The van took us back to the hotel, and we all headed to the bar. After a good steak and a couple of beers, I told Ernie to call the promoter and work it out. He set everything up and told me Frank Schramm agreed to ten rounds; we weren't going to be the main event, but I was going to be paid a great purse. So here we go again. I'm still pissed off and numb from the decision just a few hours ago, and already I agree to another fight.

After we all got drunk and filled our bellies, we went to our rooms to sleep. DeeDee tried to talk to me, tried to make some sense out of all the shit that happened tonight, but I was still too mad to listen. I hardly slept all night and before you know it, it's time to get up. I looked in the mirror and saw twelve rounds of punishment from the night before. *What an idiot.* It enraged me all over again, especially since I agreed to do it again in ten weeks. *Money, that's all it is. Give up your body and your mind for money. You're definitely never going anywhere after a draw and a loss to a chump, so what is it? Its money, that's all, you're just chasing the money now. Give up years of your life for money. That's what it comes down to.*

DeeDee backs me up on this. "Money for your family," he put it, "Take care of them. Think of them, they're counting on you."

"I know, I know," I said. I'm going to fight Schramm and knock him out like before, but then what?"

When we were back in Chicago, I got the car, headed to the South Side to DeeDee's apartment, and went down to the bar below. Everyone there told me how I got screwed again, and when we told them we were going back in a couple of months to fight Schramm, they all said I was not going to get cheated again. "Better knock him out cold, or otherwise don't be surprised!"

Since the fight, I felt awful, both mentally and physically. I had a terrible headache, which I told no one about, and mentally the loss took the heart right out of me. DeeDee kept reassuring me that everyone knew I won both of those fights. "You're gonna have to get it out of your mind.

Go home, relax, and take three, four days off. Come back to the gym ready to work."

We pounded down a few drinks and everyone around me kept encouraging me. I felt a little better mentally, but when I got in my car to leave, I hit the steering wheel five or six times and screamed. I was still mad about the decision, and I knew I would be for a while. All the way home I went through the fight round by round, punch by punch. I tried to come to some reason why the judges could give him the decision but couldn't, under any circumstances. I almost felt like crying I was so mad.

When I got home my wife gave me a hug. DeeDee had called my father after the fight and told him the outcome and that I was alright. My wife knew I had lost. When I gave her the check, she asked "How come so much?"

"That's what you get when you get fucked over in the great sport of boxing," I replied, She understood what I meant and knew I was mad, so she left me alone. She knew me well enough to know I like to be by myself when I'm pissed. I did tell her that I was going back in twelve weeks.

"Why? Don't push your luck!"

"Luck? What luck?"

"You know what I mean," and I did know, but the money was the new goal.

"It's strictly money now."

Money, the root of all evil. People steal it, kill for it, cheat others out of it. And here I was, willing to physically punish myself for it!

Chapter Eleven

I started my training for my last trip to the State of New York after about four days of rest. DeeDee even called me on the last day to see if I was coming down to the gym, thinking I might've changed my mind. I laughed and said, "I'll be down tomorrow. I've still been running the last two days. I wasn't going to quit."

"Good, I'll see you tomorrow. We're going to have a good talk and do some work." I would not be sparring for the first week or so, just working on the bags and some movement. The next day, on my drive down to the gym, the last fight started to come back in my mind. These two fights took away any chance I had to move up the ladder, so all the rest of my fights would be for money. I knew I had to put the last two fights out of my mind, but it was hard, it was consuming my mind again and soured me.

When I got to the gym, the crusty smell of sweat and leather hit my nose. I could probably be taken there blindfolded and know where I was when the door opened. I walked in, shook Ernie's and DeeDee 's hands, and Ernie led me into the office to talk before I changed. They both told me to put the fuckups out of my mind. They told me I fought two great fights, not to change anything in my style, and never take a fight for granted. Prepare the same way, and everything will work out fine. I knew they were trying to lift my spirits, but it's still very hard to forget, it's too fresh. Still, they were right, so I decided to do my best and get on with it.

I changed into my gear and we went to work. I trained hard physically for the fight, but mentally I was still having a tough time.

After six weeks of training it was time for my third trip to New York. While on the flight, DeeDee gave me the usual pep talk, adding in to put the last two fights out of my mind. By this point, I was getting sick of people telling me to forget what happened. It happened to me, not to anyone else, how do they know how I felt? That's the thing about boxing, all the people with the advice are outside of the ropes. You are the one inside the ropes giving your body and mind, doing everything in your power to stay alive. Only two men feel the brutality, you and your opponent. It's the same old thing when we landed: the same guy picked us up at the airport in the same van and took us to the boxing commission for the physical. On the way there, he was like everyone else, telling me some crap about the last two fights. All I wanted was get this over with and go home. Physical, hotel, dinner, sleep. I could barely wait for the fight. My anxiety was sky high. All I wanted was to be alone, but I couldn't let down the people on my side, who stood behind me the entire time. The next day, the driver picked us up 4:00 p.m. and took us to the arena.

I see Frank Schramm walking through the hall. He looks at least ten pounds heavier—he was never an Adonis, but he just looks sloppy now. I was worried they were going to pull a fast one and switch opponents on me, so I'm glad to see he's at least here. So far, so good. DeeDee wraps my hands, joking all the while, trying to put a smile on my face, and I start to feel better. We get the call for fight time and nobody is more relieved than me. The referee gives us our instructions and we go to our corners to wait for the bell.

The bell rings for Round One, Schramm and I meet in the center of the ring, and I throw two soft jabs, which he blocks. Then I fire three hard jabs which land right on his face. Now it's on! He knows I have power because I knocked him out two years ago. I'm so pissed off about the other fights that I just want to kill this guy. I control the round with ease and he walks back to his corner with his nose bleeding all over. DeeDee says, "Beautiful! You are the king in there, keep it up! Don't get careless." Round Two starts and I go after him again, going hard to the body then back to the head. I'm actually surprising myself I am fighting so well. Now he has a bloody nose and a swollen left eye. In Round Three, he tries to throw what he's got but my punches are hurting him. I see him wince when I hit him to the body. At the bell, I can see him shaking his head in disgust, he knows he is outgunned. DeeDee doesn't say anything between rounds; he can see what I'm doing. His eyes tell me I am doing right, just like he taught me.

Round Four starts and I am looking for the KO. I bang him everywhere. With about a minute left in the round, I knock him down with a straight right hand. He gets up and clinches, in survival mode at this point. DeeDee screams, "Now, right now, finish it!" I nod. In the fifth round Schramm backs up to the ropes, taking some hard shots, and goes down again about a minute into the round. He takes an eight count, and I am right back on him. After four or five unanswered punches he slumps down in the corner.

The referee doesn't even count, he just waves his arms, and the fight is over. A fifth-round TKO for me. Relief pours over my entire body. Fans are cheering, I'm back in the win column, and DeeDee and I have big shit-eating grins on our faces. He gives me a big hug and whispers in my ear, "Now let's get the fuck outta here."

After I shower, get dressed, and get our money, the same driver takes us back to our hotel, congratulating me all the way, and promises to pick us up early the next day so we can get home. I throw my gear in the room, and DeeDee, Ernie, and I head for the restaurant. DeeDee has his usually Crown Royal, and Ernie and I order a couple of beers. I feel like a giant weight has been lifted off my back. I am happy, I have very few bruises, and I won by a TKO, *thank God*.

We ate, drank, celebrated, and then we started to talk about my future. I felt so calm. DeeDee told me that I fought the best fight of my career. "Like a maniac, you controlled the fight after the first ten seconds all the way till the end." He told me he was always very proud of me, not just tonight. A few kind words from him were enough to make me feel like I was on top of the world. The next day, the driver took us to the airport and gave me a hug, saying he hoped I'd fight there again.

After we landed, DeeDee and I made our traditional stop in the bar. The fight was broadcast on ESPN, so when we walked in everybody congratulated me on a great fight. While we were at the bar, Ernie called to say that a promoter from Cincinnati had called him with a fight for me in Covington in eleven weeks. Ernie encouraged me to take it, and since I was feeling so good at the moment, I agreed. I had fought a great fight—three, actually, even if I only won one, so this time I felt tough and invincible.

Boxing is not just a physical sport. It takes a great psychological toll on you. All the training, all the hard work, the waiting, the thinking of the fight—it can all be too much. I made the most money in 1981 in only three fights, but the toll it took on me was overwhelming. It chips at you, like a woodpecker at a tree, but you don't ever want to give up, never want to quit, like a drug.

Chapter Twelve

I was in Covington, Kentucky, on the Fourth of July weekend in 1985. By now I was thirty-four years old and burnt out. My last fight was almost a year before, but people around me were always trying to keep me active. Richard Christmas, a promoter from Cincinnati, Ohio, who handled Ruffhouse Fisher offered me the fight. I still don't know why I agreed. The payday was only $2,500, but it was something about boxing itself that pulled me back in. It stays in your blood your whole life, you keep climbing the ladder even though you know the rungs are way out of reach. Why else would I take this fight? My prime was long gone, my body hurt, my hands hurt, and the money wasn't life changing. Your heart lies to you, it says *Maybe, just maybe you can do it*, and you don't even know what *it* is.

Covington was a beautiful city. I fought there five times, always for Richard Christmas, and loved it. 1985 was the 100th Anniversary of Covington, and the ring was in the middle of a huge park. The fights were scheduled for dusk, so the last couple of bouts would be fought when it was dark with all the lights on. After the fights, there would be a huge fireworks show.

I arrived the day before the fight with only DeeDee by my side. We'd been together nine years, and by now we knew each other like the back of our hands. He asked me why I was going to fight again, but I could not give him a good answer, I didn't know myself. When we went to the hotel, people looked at DeeDee like he was some sort of an alien because he was black. You would think by 1985 people would have been a little more educated, but this was Kentucky. I knew DeeDee didn't like coming to Covington for this reason, but he did it to be in my corner, and I wanted him there.

About 3:00 the next afternoon, someone picked us up and drove us to the venue and to get a physical. They asked me how much I weighed, and I told them about 220, but Richard said, "Make it 219. Your opponent is 200 pounds." He didn't want too much of a weight difference. In 1985, there was no cruiser weight, so anyone over 175 lbs. was a heavyweight. We didn't have dressing rooms, so we went to our tent, which I shared with Tom Fischer. I asked him, "Are you still doing this shit?"

"I was just about to ask you the very same thing," he replied. Neither one of us had a good answer. Tom put on his trunks and went to sit down when we heard a *RIIIIIIP* as he split his trunks right up the ass. "Can you believe this?" he said. Everyone was laughing. Luckily, I had an extra pair of trunks that fit him, and he said, "I owe you a beer after the fights."

"That's why you split your damn trunks," Tom's trainer said, All that beer you've been drinking."

The fights began soon after: three were four-round bouts, two were six-round bouts, and Tom and I were fighting ten-rounders. Now came the nervous part, more than the last several days, as I wondering why I took this fight to begin with. I had fought only three times in 1982, twice in '83, and once in'84. The reason was my hands and elbows were so sore that after each fight that I couldn't even brush my teeth or comb my hair. My elbows kept getting hyperextended and terrible pain shot right through to my shoulder. Now here I was again, about to fight. *I'm going to be hurting. I must be fucking crazy. I should really get my head examined.*

But it's too late now, and the call comes to enter the ring, and I'm fighting someone named Tom Persons. The ring outside is set up beautifully, and its great weather, too, about seventy-five degrees. We get instructions from the referee and go to our corners to wait for the first round. The bell rings and we're in action. Persons is about 5'11" and can't weigh more than 200 lbs., so I have a good two inches and more than twenty pounds on him—good news for me. By the middle of the first round I can also see I have a lot more experience than him. Anything can happen in a fight—lucky punches, cuts, drops in stamina—but the most I have to worry about are my hands and elbows. Up to this point, I haven't thrown a really hard punch to test my elbows or hands. And Kentucky still uses the old 8oz gloves with horsehair padding, so I hit the concrete floor to move down the padding for my knuckles to be closer to the leather.

The end of the first round, we get against the ropes and throw some bombs at each other, but the bell rings just as we really get into it. DeeDee tells me to push him back and force the fight, to use my weight to tire him out. As always, I follow his orders, and it's working great. Person's using a lot of energy to keep me back, and in the meantime I am landing my punches. My timing is way, way off, my footwork is clumsy, I don't look too good, and I'm missing more than connecting, but I feel I am winning. By the fourth round, I notice a small cut on his left eyebrow and some swelling under his left eye from my jabs. I am winning this fight, but I can't put together two or three punches to hurt him. He seems to be getting a little stronger while I'm slowing down a bit.

In the sixth round, I open a gash above his left eye and it's really starting to swell underneath. Now I can work on the eye and try to swell it shut so he can't see, and already the blood is running into his eye. Good for me. Before the seventh round, DeeDee tells me the doctor looked at him, so use the elbow trick to go for the eye. I plan to throw a left hook short and follow through with my elbow to catch him in the eye. It's a foul, but it's hard for the ref to see if you do it when he's facing your back. I can rub my thumb on his eye in the clinches to make it swell shut and the doctor would stop the fight. These are all dirty tricks, but I'm not the first or last fighter to use them.

The start of the seventh round, he comes out like a maniac. His corner must have told him he doesn't have to long to go with the bad eye. It's hard to use my dirty tricks, so I pretty much play it safe. He slows down some in the eighth round, but I am tired and my elbows hurt bad. I fight hard, landing some left hooks on his eye, and I know he can't see because he hardly moves when I throw a punch.

At the bell, I'm gassed and tell DeeDee I feel like throwing up. He gives me three big gulps of the "magic water," and I feel better almost immediately, ready to finish up the two rounds. But just as the bell rings for Round Nine, the doctor stops the fight because of Person's eye. I know how terrible this feels, and he starts arguing with the doctor, the referee, anyone who would listen, but to no avail. I didn't need the water after all.

So he lost, but did I really win? My elbows were shot, useless. I didn't feel the punches, but I looked in the mirror and saw a raccoon. Still, the fight was over and I was elated. I told DeeDee, "That's it, I'm done," and he was glad to hear it.

I waited for our money in the tent with Fischer, who had won a second-round KO. DeeDee was paid $300 in cash and was happy. I looked at my $2,500 check, thought about how I struggled the whole fight, and shook my head. *Fuck this. Never again!* This time, I meant it. This time, I was lucky.

After we changed, Tom, his trainer, DeeDee, and I went out in the park, listened to music, watched the fireworks, and proceeded to get hammered. Seven or eight years before, we both tried to kill each other in the ring, and now we were sharing a hangover. This was also Tom's last fight, so we celebrated hard. We drank to celebrate our careers and also to kill the pain of many rounds, in both fights and sparring sessions. People in the park still looked at DeeDee and Tom's trainer, who was also black, like they didn't belong, but to Tom and me they were life-long friends and confidants. Both Tom and I glared back at the assholes rolling their eyes at our much-achieved trainers, saying *Just try to pull this shit in Chicago or New York*. I told DeeDee, "Don't let these people ruin your night. Believe me, no one's got the balls to do anything." DeeDee laughed and agreed. That was the last time I saw Tom Fischer, and I hope he gets a chance to read this someday. A great way to end a career: with a fight, outside, under the lights.

The next day we were on familiar turf, Chicago. I walked DeeDee to a cab and told him again—this was definitely the end. I had said this before, but the pain in my head, elbows, and hands told me all I needed to know. I told DeeDee, "The only thing I will miss is seeing you every day, but I promise to come down to the gym a couple of times a month to see you." I gave him my word that the next time we went to the fights, we would be sitting in the crowd. DeeDee laughed and said, "I'll even buy the tickets, just don't change your mind on me."

When DeeDee passed away in about 1993, I was deeply saddened. I could picture his great smile when he liked what I was doing. I will always remember his words he would tell me between rounds: "Stay calm, cool and relaxed. If you're too tight, you'll lose all your endurance. Your muscles need to be loose and relaxed, and then everything else will fall into place." He was a great trainer and a great man. I miss the man every day. DeeDee was a quiet man, but he got his message across, and he knew boxing like the back of his hand. He and I were perfect for each other: two humble men trying to reach one goal.

Chapter Thirteen

Later that year, Richard Christmas sent in a request to the director of Capital Wrestling Corp., Robert James Morella (a.k.a wrestler Gorilla Monsoon), to see if he would be interested in making me a pro wrestler. After all, I had a name from boxing, and I also wrestled in high school—Greco-Roman wrestling, with rules, but I wasn't a complete rookie. I sent in my resume, thinking nothing would come of it, but about three weeks later I get a call from Gorilla Monsoon himself! He tells me they have a show at the Amphitheatre in about a month, so if I'm interested I should see him before the matches start.

Did I really want to do this? I knew there would be a lot of travel involved, and this was the one thing I really didn't want to do. My wife didn't really want me to get back in the ring. More injuries, more pounding on my body, did I really need this? But I figured it wouldn't hurt to see him before the matches. He reserved two tickets for me at the box office, so I called DeeDee Armor and told him that Kip and I would pick him to check this wrestling thing out.

"Are you out of your mind?" DeeDee said. "I thought you were done fighting!"

"This stuff is all an act, how bad could it be for me?" DeeDee agreed to come along, but all the way there he keeps telling me that if I still want to fight I should stick to what I know best, boxing.

When we got to the Amphitheatre and go to the box office, I asked for the tickets that were left for me and told the guy behind the counter that I brought another friend as well, would there be any chance of getting another ticket? He said, "For you, my friend, absolutely," and handed me the extra ticket. Just goes to show, it pays a little to be known in the city. When we got in, I sought out Mike Gilenna, the Illinois Athletic Director at the time, and told him what's going on. He told me he'd introduce me and came back in a few minutes with a 6'5", 350-lb. guy: Monsoon. He looked at me and led me back to his office.

First thing he said is that I was too skinny and he wanted me to put on twenty or twenty-five pounds. I sort of smiled at that and said, "I 'm in great shape right now, why would I want to put on twenty-five pounds?"

"We'll give you something to put the weight on, all muscle."

"You mean steroids?"

"Something like that. All these guys use it, and they're all strong as bulls." I told him I'd think about it and get back to him in a few days. "Fine, here's how it works. You would train for two months in Minnesota with some other guys. You would be paid, and you wouldn't have to spend a cent." I told him it sounded great, but again, I needed to think about it. Kip, DeeDee, and I walked around the dressing room for a couple more minutes and then we went to our seats.

The main event that night was Hulk Hogan versus some nobody, so everyone already knew he was going to win the match. The second main feature was Sgt. Slaughter, dressed as an all-American drill sergeant, versus the Iron Sheik, who represented someplace like the Middle East. The Hulk was 6'5" at best, but they always said he was 6'8. The wrestlers wore wrestling boots with an inch-and-a-half rubber sole to make them look bigger than life. Sgt. Slaughter beat the Sheik, and Hulk Hogan almost beheaded his opponent but to be honest, the rest of the show was all boring bullshit—fake as could be, very predictable, and not too much fun.

After the show, the three of us made our way to the bar beneath DeeDee's apartment and talked about all the pros and cons of wrestling for me. Kip says, "What about your job?" *Good point. What was I going to do, take a leave of absence? I might never get my job back.* DeeDee says "I know you don't want to take steroids to put on twenty pounds.

72

Forget all this crap. It was an idea, but I know it's not for you." *Agreed.* We all voted unanimously that this wasn't for me. We had a few more drinks, something to eat, and some good laughs about the show. On the way home, my mind was made up. Good guy vs. bad guy, obvious winners and losers. It was nothing like boxing.

That Monday, I called Monsoon and thanked him for the opportunity, but I'd had all I want to do with the ring. "No problem," he said. If you change your mind, let me know. I'm interested in having you."

Chapter Fourteen

After six years as an amateur and eight years as a pro, I was done. There's a lot that I miss, but also a I'd like to forget. Boxing is like being bi-polar, only up or down, very little in between. One thing I learned was that 95% of people involved in the fight world will lie right to your face and not lose a minute of sleep over it.. It's the managers and trainers that tend to be shady, not the fighters. I was lucky to have DeeDee and Ernie with me after my first manager and trainer were caught stealing from my pockets. When I confronted them, they just lied more. But what they forgot was who they were lying to, so I gave them a little lesson and took whatever money they had on them right then and there. I said goodbye and never looked back, although, to this day, I get pissed every time I think about how my so-called friends stole from me. I was brought up to be loyal to my friends and will do anything for someone who I feel is a loyal friend to me, but there's not many of those people in the boxing world.

Knowing all I know, I would never let anyone in my family or a good friend get involved in this sport. The sheer misery of losing a fight and getting your ass kicked in front of everyone who knows and loves you is difficult to take. The pressure of each fight takes its toll on the best of men. Fighters have their own little brotherhood of respect and friendship. Any man brave enough to step into the ring should be respected.

Now that my career is over it's very difficult to describe my feelings. I made a lot of good friends, but I also lost respect for some people. I know I will miss boxing, and it's a tough call, but you have to get out when it's time. I believe that boxing is something within you, in your blood, but when the time comes to quit you must make the smart choice. You have the ring tugging at your heartstrings, *Just one more, one more*, but your head knows there can be no more. Your body has taken enough. Your brain has taken enough. They say all good things come to an end, but is boxing really a good thing? Neither I nor anyone else ever realized how I would suffer. Not then, not years later. It really all started with Jimmy Cross, a fight that has stuck with me for over thirty-five years.

In June of 1978, at Holy Cross High School in River Grove, I was scheduled to fight Donny Martin, an orthodox (right-handed fighter) heavyweight like me. It was going to be my first scheduled ten-rounder, so I trained harder than I ever had before. I got up every morning at four, ran for a full hour, usually about seven miles, then go home to do sit ups, leg raises, and ab work. I was in great shape and knew I could easily go ten rounds with no problem. About three days before the fight, we got a call that Donny suffered a cut in training and would not be able to fight, but it wouldn't be a problem because a substitute fighter was training for another fight in June.

When you're sparring in the gym you're mostly relaxed, there's no crowd and you're pretty familiar with whom you are sparring with. You're comfortable with your surroundings. It's a whole different ball game when it comes to the real thing. Your nerves get on edge a few days before the fight, and you want to be done with all the training and just go. Those last few days are really the worst part.

When I walked into the locker room I instantly smelled the stale odor of sweat from the unwashed gym clothes the kids never took home. I was the main event, so I had a private room and some time to kill during the preliminaries. DeeDee came in soon after to wrap my hands. This is a very important part of his job: wrapping them correctly is the difference between risking injury that could hinder the rest of a boxer's career. DeeDee did a great job, as always, and the boxing commissioner came to check and initial them. Fifteen minutes before the fight, I limbered up by shadowboxing and hitting my mitts on DeeDee's hands. When I was done, my manager came into the dressing room and said there was another change, that I would be fighting Jimmy Cross, and that two different guys will be working my corner instead of my regular corner guys, Frank Martin and Tommy Casey. I knew why, he wanted to set up for another project with these guys to make himself some money. He made this decision for himself, for his own personal gain. We argued, but it's too late.

We get the call to head towards the ring. As we walk down the hall, my manager and I are still arguing about my corner men. This is not the time to be distracted. I need to be clear headed and focused only on the fight. But at this point, whatever is done is done.

We enter the ring, so many friends and family are there cheering for me like crazy. I'm moving around the ring, shadowboxing and warming up, when out of the corner of my eye I see Jimmy Cross doing the same. To my surprise, he's a southpaw, left-handed. I'm absolutely shocked because I have never fought a southpaw, only sparred with one *maybe* once or twice over a year ago. I tell my manager, but he just replies, "So what?"

I don't have much time to argue. "So what?! So now it's a whole different ball game!" Next thing I know, the bell rings for Round One. I yell to everyone in my corner, "Where's my mouthpiece?" Nobody can find it. I scream at my manager that there's already a problem with these new guys. "Give me my fucking mouthpiece!" The ref comes over and says he'll call the fight if I don't come out. So here I go—no mouthpiece, fighting a southpaw, in for the fight.

The first half of the round, we mostly feel each other out before we get to fighting. About five seconds before the bell rings, I knock him down with a straight right hand, but he's more surprised than hurt. I go back to my corner, screaming again, "Where's my fucking mouthpiece?" The two idiots in my corner still can't find it. Ding for Round Two. About two minutes into the round, Cross lands a vicious left hand to my right eye and splits my right eyebrow in half. The blood is running into my eye and it's hard to see, but soon I hear the bell. I go back to my corner and, believe it or not, someone lost the coagulant that slows down the blood flow. Plus, still no mouthpiece. The bell rings for Round Three, and the boxing becomes a savage fight, a flat out brawl. He's bleeding from a cut between his nose and eyebrow from my left hook. I'm bleeding like crazy from the cut over eye, and my lips are chewed up from no mouth piece. Nothing in my corner can stop the cut from bleeding and they can't find the mouthpiece. I can hardly believe what's going on.

The bell rings for Round Four, and I know I have to fight hard or else the doctor might stop the fight because of the cut. My white trunks are now pink, soaked with my own blood. Towards the end of the round, Cross throws a right uppercut that catches me under the chin and cuts me. The cut isn't big but it's bleeding enough to make my face a bloody mess, and I'm glad to hear the bell end the round. It's *Groundhog Day* in my corner. I'm swollen and shredded. No coagulant. No mouthpiece. Now the doctor looks at my cuts and tells me I better do something fast or he's going to stop the fight—in other words, knock Jimmy Cross out.

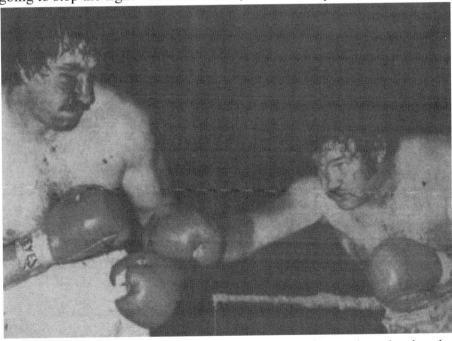

Fifth round, I go out like a man possessed and start throwing bombs from all angles. My right eye is useless, so I'm throwing all I got and connecting, but he stays up. In the clinch I notice he is bleeding from both ears and I know he's on his way out. Punch after punch lands on both of us. The crowd is on their feet screaming, loving every minute, waiting for one fighter to kill the other. Like in NASCAR, they're waiting for a crash. Who cares about either of us? They love the blood. The more, the better.

Just when I think I have him, the round ends. The doctor takes a look at my right eye, which now has a cut more than two and a half inches long and open half an inch, and says that he can't let me go out for the next round. I'm pleading with him for one more round, saying "Look, both of his ears are bleeding! He has to be hurt badly! Why won't you let me fight? He's hurt way worse than I am." He doesn't give in. The fight is over.

As I leave the ring, still bleeding, I look for my manager and the corner men. *Gone. They are gone.* The only one is DeeDee I asked him what the fuck happened, and he tells me the other guys wouldn't let him near the ring, physically pushed an old man out of the way. I'm in the dressing room, trying to process what just happened, and in walks a friend of mine with my mouthpiece, which he found after the match sitting in the second row. Then the doctor came in to stitch me up: twenty-two stitches above my right eye, six under my chin. By now my right eye is almost swollen shut, and he tells DeeDee that I probably have a concussion. Don't let him sleep too long, try and keep him awake. *What a joke*, I think, *DeeDee lives thirty miles away.* For all this shit, my cut is $3,000.

This story, this fight, has been with me every single day since then. After Jimmy Cross, I had a nine-fight winning streak and got myself ranked up to #9, but still that loss stayed with me. The cuts I suffered to my face, the confusion of that day. It was early in my career, but slowly, surely my heart and desire for the sport began to dwindle.

Because of that fight, the loss, the confusion, and many concussions from before and after that night, I suffer from PTSD, traumatic brain injury, REM behavior disorder excessive fatigue, daytime memory loss. I lose things, I get up from my chair and can't remember why, I lose my train of thought right in the middle of a sentence, my left hand shakes, I have angry outbursts over nothing. And I have been diagnosed with early stage Parkinson's. But the nightmares are the worst.

Nightmare after horrendous nightmare, I fight more in my sleep than I ever did in the ring. Almost every night my wife, who can no longer sleep in the same bed, has to tap my feet with a broomstick or yell my name over and over to wake me from the terrible nightmares of that day, of that fight. It never goes away, with violent movements and thrashing about. My wife can hear me yelling, "Where's my mouthpiece?" and I knock over anything in my reach. Sometimes I even sleepwalk, get up and move around the room like I'm in the ring. When she finally gets me awake, if I don't do something like drink or eat, I go right back to sleep, I'll go right back to that same nightmare, sometimes two or three times a night.

We are still together after forty-three years of marriage, with three beautiful, smart children and four grandchildren. I was very, very lucky to have married Ellen, an angel—no other woman in the world would stick with a pure self-centered asshole like myself. No one likes to see their, son, husband, or father bruised up. It's easy to imagine what my family is going through from my current mental state. My wife has the most to do, and now after all of the things wrong with me, it's twice as hard. The little money I made from fighting has not set us up in any great financial means. Now I'm on disability so I cannot work. I feel terrible about the situation I've put my wife in, and every man in some sort of similar situation knows how this feels.

What we know now that we didn't then is the damage that is caused to the brain from punches. A whiplash effect, when the brain bounces back and forth against the skull and bruises, and eventually the cells die from constant bruising. It's called Chronic Traumatic Encephalopathy, a degenerative disease found in people who have suffered repeated blows to the head, formerly known as "punch-drunk" in boxers. The damage is permanent. Concussion after concussion, I still fought on, never realizing the effects it would have later in my life. Nightmares, punching the pillow, knocking over the night stand, even punching myself. I can't get a restful night's sleep because my brain just doesn't stop. It's a never-ending battle, night after night, as I relive some of my fights in my sleep and I wake up exhausted and have to take meds to deal with it all. Because of all the hype and recognition football players received about their frequent concussions, I called the Illinois Boxing Commission to see if they could help me financially with all the meds I take. To date, they haven't returned any of my calls. I did get to speak with someone in the sports field who told me that football has a union, which is why players can get the physical and financial support they need, while boxing has no union. Plus, because fights are held in different states and injuries can build gradually, there's no way to determine which state would be responsible for covering an injury or its aftermath.

This is what people don't understand, all the head shots you take day in and day out, sparring with world class fighters for six, seven, eight, nine rounds a day. Even with head gear and bigger gloves, the thuds on your head start to add up. People think the damage a fighter sustains comes from the actual fight, but much of the damage to a fighter's head and torso comes from sparring every day. This might come to half a million punches to the head in every fighter's career. It's no wonder fighters end up with PTSD, poor balance, slurred speech, memory problems, sleep disorders, depression, and Parkinson's. It's all inevitable. Parkinson's disease robs people of the control over their movements, starting with tremors or uncontrollable shaking (mostly in the hands) then with shuffling instead of walking, stiff limbs, bad balance, and slurred speech. The shuffling gait used to be called punch-drunk in fighters that caught too many punches to the head. All those punches in fights and sparring take a toll on your head. So this could be why fighters or boxers end up all fucked up at the end of their careers.

This, I have experienced firsthand. I have suffered from depression for many years. I don't like to attend many social events because I'm always on edge, calm one minute and red hot the next for no reason. I walk down the street as though I am drunk because my balance is very screwed up and I drift from side to side instead of straight.

I read an article in the *New York Times* how no-contact boxing was good for those suffering from Parkinson's. The writer, Dan Kiefer, diagnosed with Parkinson's at thirty-five years old, took up boxing training. Using the heavy bag, speed bag, and focus mitts helped improve his hand-eye coordination and balance, and jumping rope, walking, and using stationary bikes increased his stamina and strengthened his heart. Since reading the article, I have hung the heavy bag back up in the garage. It feels good to hit the bag again, and using all my energy in a workout means I don't have as much left for depression and anger.

Boxing is the cause—but maybe training could be the solution, too.

Chapter Fifteen

There was a time I was on the front page of the *Chicago Sun-Times*, *Chicago Tribune*, and *The Daily News*. Sometimes I got full page coverage. This was even before I started to fight for Ernie. Don't get me wrong, I'm not saying I was some great champion, but my fights in Chicago could easily fill the Aragon or the Amphitheatre, or any other place I fought. Any white heavyweight draws attention, and I had a great following, which Ernie loved and turned into good publicity. Now, it's as if I was never there. All those so-called followers leave after a couple of losses.

When you're on top, people love to be around a winner, they want to be connected. *George is my cousin. George is my childhood friend. I was in the Army with George. We played football together. We worked together. We went to kindergarten together*—everyone tries to claim you as their own. When you're on your way out, it's a totally different story. No one even bothers to call anymore.

I had my so-called fifteen minutes of fame, and I had a lot of fun. I made a few bucks and some good friends, guys who put in endless hours to teach the trade for very little money but for the love of the sport. I have some great memories. I did something very few individuals do, and I would do it again. When I look back, there is nothing like a crowd of eight thousand people screaming and cheering for you. The exhilaration is inexplicable, adrenaline is pumping, and you're ready to get on with the fight. The thrill of sweet victory and raising your arms for a win is a rush

84

you'll never get over or get anywhere else. It is the most rewarding feeling you will ever know, an accomplishment achieved on your own through dedication, hard work, and perseverance. No drug could ever come close to this euphoria. I fought the World Heavyweight Champ, and no one can ever take that away. Screw the disease. I have something very few people have ever known: the thrill of victory and the agony of defeat. I trained hard, fought hard, and whether I won or lost, I earned respect. There are no teammates, no substitutes, no taking a time-out—just you, alone. No athlete trains or takes punishment the way a boxer does.

When I started fighting amateur, my goal was to be the heavyweight champ. To me, this was better than being elected President of the United States. Boxing is no longer the sport I knew forty years ago. With only one champion in each division, it was the greatest achievement of all world sports. Now there are four boxing organizations—W.B.C., W.B.A., W.B.O., and I.B.F.—and the weight divisions are so watered down that each has its own champions. Splitting the weight divisions means making more money for each fight on TV. It's all for the money.

The pain, the punishment, the Parkinson's—I loved it then, and I would do it all again.

THE **GOOD**...

THE **BAD**...

...AND THE **NOW**

68607220R00051

Made in the USA
San Bernardino, CA
06 February 2018